MURAD WILFRI

C000231115

JOURNEY TO ISLAM

Diary of a German Diplomat
(1951–2000)

THE ISLAMIC FOUNDATION

Acknowledgment

The author is indebted to Mr. William Young for his editorial comments on the manuscript.

Published by

THE ISLAMIC FOUNDATION,

Markfield Conference Centre,
Ratby Lane, Markfield,
Leicester LE67 9SY, United Kingdom
Main Building - Tel: (01530) 244944/5, Fax: (01530) 244946
Publications - Tel: (01530) 249230, Fax: (01530) 249656
E-Mail: i.foundation@islamic-foundation.org.uk
Publications E-Mail: publications@islamic-foundation.com
Website: www.islamic-foundation.org.uk

Quran House, P.O. Box 30611, Nairobi, Kenya

P.M.B. 3193, Kano, Nigeria

British Library Cataloguing-in-Publication Data
A Catalogue record for this book is available from the British Library

ISBN 0-86037-326-6

Typeset by: N.A. Qaddoura
Cover Design: Nasir Cadir

Printed by Antony Rowe Ltd, Chippenham, Wiltshire.

بِسْمِ اللهِ الرَّحْمَنِ الرَّحِيمِ

ٱلَّذِينَ كَفَرُواْ وَصَدُّواْ عَن سَبِيلِ ٱللَّهِ أَضَلَّ أَعْمَلَهُمْ ۝ وَٱلَّذِينَ
ءَامَنُواْ وَعَمِلُواْ ٱلصَّلِحَتِ وَءَامَنُواْ بِمَا نُزِّلَ عَلَىٰ مُحَمَّدٍ وَهُوَ ٱلْحَقُّ مِن
رَّبِّهِمْ كَفَّرَ عَنْهُمْ سَيِّئَاتِهِمْ وَأَصْلَحَ بَالَهُمْ ۝ ذَٰلِكَ بِأَنَّ ٱلَّذِينَ كَفَرُواْ
ٱتَّبَعُواْ ٱلْبَطِلَ وَأَنَّ ٱلَّذِينَ ءَامَنُواْ ٱتَّبَعُواْ ٱلْحَقَّ مِن رَّبِّهِمْ كَذَٰلِكَ يَضْرِبُ
ٱللَّهُ لِلنَّاسِ أَمْثَلَهُمْ ۝

(محمد 1-3)

*In the name of God, the Most Gracious,
the Dispenser of Grace*

*As for those who are bent on denying the truth and on barring others
from the path of God – all their good deeds will He let go to waste;
whereas those who have attained to faith and do righteous deeds, and
have come to believe in what has been bestowed from on high upon
Muḥammad – for it is the truth from their Sustainer – shall attain to
God's Grace. He will efface their past bad deeds, and will set their
hearts at rest. This, because those who are bent on denying the truth
pursue falsehood, whereas those who have attained to faith pursue but
the truth from their Sustainer. In this way God sets forth unto men
the parables of their true state.*

Muḥammad, 47:1–3
(translation by Muhammad Asad)

To my fellow Muslims
in the West

Contents

◆ Bonn, 11 September 1980
Muslim in spite of myself   47
◆ Bonn, 25 September 1980
Lā ilāha illallāh, Muḥammad rasūlullāh   48
◆ Bonn, 26 September 1980
Why not quadruplicity?   49
◆ Bonn, 9 October 1980
The whirling dervishes of Konya   50
◆ Bonn, 26 February 1981
The immunity of Islam   52
◆ Bonn, 12 March 1981
Muslim international law   55
◆ Istanbul, 1 August 1981
Haute couture scandal   57
◆ Bonn, 28 April 1982
Ibn Khaldūn, not Marx   59
◆ Bonn, 19 May 1982
Sunnī versus Shī'ī   62
◆ Iznik, 21 July 1982
The First Council of Nicaea   65
◆ Bursa, 22 July 1982
A church is not a mosque   67
◆ Bonn, 19 September 1982
Too good to be true?   68
◆ LH 624, 18 December 1982
Alcohol-nicotine-pork society   69
◆ Jeddah, 18 December 1982
Islamic brotherhood   71
◆ Makkah, 20 December 1982
Pilgrimage to Makkah   72
◆ Makkah, 20 December 1982
Straight back to Abraham   74

Foreword

The predicament of modern man may be summed up in a few words: we have learned to fly in the skies like birds and to swim in the oceans like fish, but we have yet to learn to live on the earth as good human beings. Man's search to learn to live as a good human being poses the greatest challenge for mankind in the new millennium. The 20th century was remarkable for its achievements in the fields of science, technology and development. Yet it was also the most violent century of human history, annihilating over 100 million human beings in two world wars and over two hundred localized conflicts. Despite two centuries of unprecedented economic development, over 40% of the human race lives in poverty and some 20% in abject poverty, while 87% of the world's GDP (Gross Domestic Product) is owned and controlled by twenty countries, with only 18% of the world's population. Is the 21st century going to be any better? This question prompts no easy answer.

Easy answers could be deceptive. However, as giving up the search would inevitably lead to nihilism and doom, looking for alternatives is the only real option. Stories of people who have chosen to engage in such a quest abound, but they often succeed only in providing a partial consolation to what otherwise appears as a dismal horizon. Among those who have undertaken this search assiduously and have been able to see some light beyond the tunnel are two German intellectuals –

Leopold Weiss (Muhammad Asad) and Murad Wilfried Hofmann. The stories of their search are told in two very different styles. Whereas Asad's *Road to Macca* is the moving odyssey of a turbulent soul's rendezvous with destiny during the first half of the 20th century, Murad Hofmann's *Diary*, which covers the second half of the century, belongs to a different genre. Its insights are illuminating, for they unveil the throbbing of a heart and the longings of a soul seeking truth in a world haunted by poverty in plenty, despair in prosperity, and dislocation despite progress. The subtle flashes of light that radiate from the pages of this *Diary* agitate the mind and move the soul.

It was a pleasure to read it as I was preparing to welcome Dr. Murad Hofmann in Islamabad as our first speaker at the Khurram Murad Memorial Lecture in February 2000. I was very unhappy to learn that the book had been out of print for quite some time, and am therefore doubly grateful that brother Murad Hofmann so readily consented to update the *Diary* and give the Islamic Foundation the opportunity to publish it. Hence this new edition.

I feel honoured to contribute this Foreword to a book so rich in insights and reflections on the world in which we live today, and so revealing of the myriad of milestones in a journey to Islam. It is not merely the diary of one person; it is a chronicle of our times and may be a pointer to the future.

Leicester   **Khurshid Ahmad**
20 October 2000
22nd Rajab 1421

Preface

The remarkable insights revealed in this diary throw light upon the author's approach to Islam – a process spread over many years, culminating in his definitive conversion in 1980.

As Murad Hofmann points out, the pages of this book represent no more than "a dialogue with himself", arising from a German intellectual's intense preoccupation with problems of ethics, morality and aesthetics.

Repelled by the materialism of modern technological civilization as well as by the sterility of Western sociological thought and its implied denial of all value of the question of man's spiritual destiny, Murad Hofmann appears at first to have been driven, as it were, towards a discovery of the harmony between the art-forms of the Muslim world and the religious outlook of its people. This discovery, in time, revealed to him the intimate connection between Muslim culture and the Islamic faith as such.

Spurred on by his experiences as a diplomat and traveller in various Muslim countries – predominantly in North Africa and Turkey – he immersed himself in a study of the Qur'ān and, over the years, came to realize that an acceptance of Islam was the only logical conclusion of his search for the ultimate truth of life. Thereupon he adopted the name Murad, which signifies "purpose" – that is to say, the innermost purpose of the life of Wilfried Hofmann.

There is no doubt that the "diary" displayed in the following pages will substantially contribute to a better appreciation of Islam by those Westerners who still view this religion of ours with a suspicion amounting to animosity, and who stubbornly refuse even to contemplate the possibility of a truly Divine revelation after the time of Jesus and moreover, a revelation which because of its clearness and simplicity, is essentially different from the picturesque theology of the Bible and from the religious experiences of the West.

Lisbon   **Muhammad Asad**
December 1985

Introduction

If one is ignorant of a matter one easily becomes opposed to it.
(Citation attributed to 'Alī ibn Abī Ṭālib)

It seems easier to explain what this diary is not, than to describe what it is. Certainly, it does not record a convert's psycho-dramatic "confession", nor does it attempt to scrutinize what cannot be analyzed: the fully integrated emotional and cognitive elements motivating a change of religion. This diary does not either provide a chronological biography, even if it faithfully reflects concrete events – as in Makkah and Madinah. Rather this book mirrors specific stages of a mental process toward embracing Islam that was nourished by a limited number of key experiences. It was a process in which deeply rooted personal affinities for aesthetic and cultural components of Islam, its civilization and philosophy, played a major role.

Diplomats are often envied for being able to absorb foreign cultures, if only from the sidelines. To really penetrate a foreign culture is, however, both emotionally and intellectually a much further reaching proposition. It implies an adventure: the grasping from within of the very foundation of a civilization, namely, its religion.

A convert to Islam will inevitably see his own country in a "new light". This in turn will force him into a dialogue with himself. Yes, this is the subject of this book.

Brussels
Summer 1986

Murad Wilfried Hofmann

Self-fulfilling prophecies

Schenectady, N.Y., 17 May 1951

For a year now, I have been studying sociology at Union College, near the Mohawk River in up-State New York. The school's approach to the subject is rigidly empirical. Research into man's social functions and behavioural patterns does not proceed from philosophically or theologically established images of man's essential nature and purpose; value judgments are banned as "unscientific" in favour of quantifiable aspects. Man and woman, in their social interaction, are counted and measured. Their entire function and role in life is exclusively seen in terms of social integration and usefulness. This accords with the popular view of Sigmund Freud's psychology of the individual and the prevailing materialistic, mechanistic concept of life and intelligence. This behaviouristic approach is similar to the method applied by Karl von Frisch when determining the I.Q. and hereditary habits of bees.

Years before Vance Pakard's *The Pyramid Climbers*, *The Sexual Wilderness*, *The Hidden Persuaders* and Konrad Lorenz' *On Aggression*, we discovered the "laws" governing all human activity and society. However, we are not yet aware of the normative impact of sociological research: the more people read about what is "normal" according to statistical data, the more they tend to adapt to this norm. Sociology is a self-fulfilling prophecy! Indeed, my fellow students at Psi Upsilon Fraternity

3

are virtually obsessed with an urge to appear normal, well adapted and "with it".

Such an approach to human reality is obviously incompatible with an anthropology grounded in philosophy. It is equally apparent that sociological agnosticism in the disguise of behavioural science was bound to alienate people from the traditional web of autonomous ethics that undergrids society.

Nothing could better illustrate this systematic breakdown of moral barriers than the blatant sexual athleticism cultivated in the student environment to which I belong. If conformity – "keeping up with the Joneses" – is perceived as the most desirable goal of man's social and economic activities, everything, including truth, becomes relative. From then on, man wishes to do what others expect him to do. "Man without character" (Georg Simmel), man with a purely sociological conscience, is born.

This kind of sociology claims to be un-ideological, even hostile to ideology. In reality, however, it is a pseudo-religion hiding behind the trappings of fallaciously pristine natural science. Indeed, is it not highly ideological to ridicule or to refuse to ask the fundamental questions about man – Whence? Why? Wherefore? – that all serious philosophers and theologians, all through the ages, could not avoid asking.

A sociologically inspired pedagogy that seeks uniformity at the lowest common denomination, is it not the product of a world view, a *Weltanschauung*? It certainly is, for this brand of sociology prefabricates its results. For it, atheism is not only a working hypothesis but is axiomatic. However, if this is to become the world perspective of Americans, then it will also be so in Europe. How are we to cope with a pseudo-religion like "scientific" Marxism if we, too, elevate atheism to a way of life, exposing the Western value system to the effects of unmitigated agnosticism, and hence value neutralism?

Accidents one does not survive

Holly Springs, Mississippi, 28 June 1951

Hitch-hiking for two weeks, and carrying little more than my outfit for working as a waiter (or at least bus boy), I had already travelled from Northern New York State via New Jersey and South Carolina to Florida and back up to Georgia. We expected any minute now to reach Memphis, Tennessee. I already dreamed of walking across the Mississippi Bridge there.

Then, out of nowhere, a shadow appeared right in front of us. The driver next to me jerked his foot off the accelerator. But there was no braking, on either side.

The next day, under the headline "Head-on Collision", the local newspaper reported that drunkards had crossed the highway into the on-coming traffic. Looking me over in the hospital, doctors diagnosed a broken upper jaw, a mutilated lower lip, and nineteen teeth knocked out. My right arm was dislocated, and there was a deep hole in my right knee – but I had suffered neither brain concussion nor psychological shock.

The two Chevrolets had collided frontally at a combined speed of roughly 95 mph. If I had jumped from the 5th floor of a tall building my chances of survival would have been about the same.

While the surgeon tried to re-arrange my torn face, he wondered aloud how I might have looked before. With a head movement I managed to indicate that he could find my passport in my torn jeans. For some time, the doctor alternately studied my passport photograph and my disjointed facial traits, only to mutter with some hesitation that I could always undergo aesthetic surgery after a few years...

Then, while giving me a morphine shot for the first hospital night, the surgeon shook his head and said, somewhat ceremoniously, "Dear fellow, one doesn't survive accidents like that! God must have something in store for you."

Twenty-nine years later, on 25 September 1980, I understood.

Pictures diminish fantasy

Granada/Cordoba, 7 July 1958

Even renowned German experts on Islamic art and architecture – Ernst Kühnel, Katharina Otto-Dorn, Alfred Renz – find it unusually difficult to define their subject. Oleg Grabar's majority view is that Islamic artists were so eclectic due to their personal background and contacts with the cultures of Syria, Byzantium, Persia and the Turkic tribes, that only a single element, namely the decorative use of Arabic script, can be regarded as a peculiar trademark of Islamic art styles. Yet, even children have an unerring way of spotting Islamic artefacts as belonging to a specific category.

There is, of course, no art movement (including Gothic) that started from scratch. Thus, Islamic art knew no "zero hour" but absorbed elements as it developed. Nevertheless, Islam is a religion capable of translating specific aspects of faith into principles of aesthetics.

It is therefore true that Islamic architecture, landscaping and interior decoration, in spite of their great variety, provoke a distinct Islamic spatial feeling, reaching from the grandiose to the intimate. This can, for instance, be experienced in the Alhambra building and courtyards at Granada, or in characteristic mosques such as those in Cordoba, Kairouan, Cairo and Istanbul – in the latter, particularly the Süleymaniye, Sultan Ahmet, Rüstem Pasha and Sokollu Mehmet Pasha mosques. The same is true of the Alhambra gardens and the Ḥaram area in Makkah.

Several elements are concretely responsible for the distinct Islamic quality of this art experience:

1. The ideal of modesty in external appearance, which governs Islamic palaces in much the same way as beautiful Muslim women wear a veil when leaving the house;
2. The democratic, anti-hierarchical structure of Islam, which also governs the layout of prayer rooms;
3. The high degree of abstraction, which is in keeping with the non-anthropomorphic Islamic image of God;
4. The human dimensions in architectural proportions, which reflect Islamic concerns with balance, sobriety, and a middle-of-the road approach to all subjects;
5. The anti-magical airiness of rooms used for ritual prayer, which demonstrates the absence of liturgy, sacraments and mysteries in Islam;
6. The shaping of gardens, following the Qur'ānic descriptions of paradise.

To find oneself in such spaces inspires a sense of elation (in the full sense of the word). He who cannot pray in a mosque will not learn to pray in a cathedral.

The absence of any kind of representations of human persons or, oh horror, God, in an Islamic environment is less due to Qur'ānic prescriptions than to the fear of fetishism and idolatry. Abstraction, as in the form of endlessly interwoven arabesques, helps the mind to concentrate on the indescribable, undefinable, unfathomable, untouchable: God.

Illustrations are not a useful tool for enriching our metaphysical imagination. On the contrary, they limit our fantasy.

Tolerance as self-abnegation

R ight in the middle of my final exams at Harvard Law School, I am getting married, for simplicity's sake, in the Harvard Chapel and by a Unitarian minister. His pre-matrimony counselling had been limited to asking whether I was certain I was free of any latent homosexual tendencies.

Above the altar, there is a frieze with the names, in this order, of Buddha, Confucius, Jesus, Moses and Mohammed. Such religious eclecticism – something for everybody! – I find rather amusing: tolerance to the point of self-abnegation. But not entirely. Historical sequence had been tampered with in order to place Jesus graphically in the centre. Ironically, by the same token, this arrangement visually underlines that Muḥammad had been the last of the prophets and therefore their "seal".

Instead of pondering all of this symbolism, I should have paid better attention to the intricacies of ancient English wedding formulae. When asked to repeat "And I plight Thee my troth" I promptly started stuttering.

God's own language?

In the bar of the oasis' only hotel, I happen to sit next to a man from this Mozabite region. While he suffers from the chilly air-conditioning (in spite of his heavy woollen *burnus*), we make small talk, carefully avoiding a discussion of the wretched Algerian war outside.

But when I mention that I had just finished reading the Qur'ān in French translation (O. Pesle/Ahmad Tidjani, *Le Coran*, Paris 1954), my neighbour becomes tight-lipped and even sinister. It now dawned upon me that he, adhering to the strict Mozabite interpretation of Islam, saw me as being involved in a sacrilege – the sacrilege committed by those who tamper with God's message that was received by Muḥammad from the angel Gabriel in Arabic, and no other language.

Witnessing such a violent reaction to a mere translating effort, I began to understand another observation I had made while walking the narrow, windy streets of Ghardaia. Indeed, through the open windows of Qur'ānic schools, I had heard shrill children's voices chanting Qur'ānic verses in Arabic – a language these little Berber kids could hardly decipher and certainly could not speak.

Such insistence on safeguarding the Qur'ān in its Arabic original is not at all primitive. Quite the contrary. It makes good sense if one accepts that the Qur'ān embodies God's very own message as delivered complete and authentic. And as such, the Qur'ān's status far surpasses that of any other text, including any part of the compilation known as the New Testament. It is the difference between first-hand and second-hand literature.

Against this background, and given the sad experiences made during the process of translating the Gospel from Aramaic via Greek and Latin into English, French or German, is it so amazing that Muslims treat even the smallest excerpts of the Qur'ānic original with reverence, touching it only with clean hand *and* body?

One should also be aware of the fact that Islamic philosophers, knowing their Aristotle, had deduced early on that, as God was Eternal, Perfect, Immovable and All-Knowing, His message (word/*logos*), too, must have existed throughout eternity, even before being revealed and thus "appearing" in human history. This question – whether the Qur'ān has been created or is essentially uncreated – once divided Islamic scholars in much the same way as their Christian colleagues were split over the question of the createdness or eternal existence of the world.

Even so, it is not necessary to believe, naïvely, that God's language is Arabic. Muḥammad received the Qur'ānic revelation in this language for the simple reason that he – an Arab preaching among Arabs – understood no other. Nor is there any valid reason to consider a translation of the Book as sacrilegious, as long as the translation is not presented as a replacement of, or as an equivalent to, the original. For this reason, translations made by Muslims usually appear under titles such as "The Meaning of the Qur'ān" and reproduce the Arabic text and its translation side by side.

It is a good question whether, after so many attempts, someone will achieve a fully "identical" translation of the Qur'ān. Much speaks against it.

Alcohol for Germany

Some of my countrymen, prospecting for oil in the Algerian stone desert, are about to lose nerve; some are even threatening to evacuate camp. No wonder: the war of liberation keeps creeping closer, and after the expected retreat of the French guards, there may be a massacre.

The German Consul General in Algiers, Siegfried von Nostitz, therefore instructs me to improve their morale with the help of two boxes of whisky: Oil for Germany!

In a terrible storm, and accompanied by the director of the German petroleum company, I fly across the Atlas Mountains in a shaky DC-3 of World War II vintage. The whisky boxes lie on the floor next to my seat. Unlike me, they are not fastened into place by a seat belt. I try, in vain, to keep them down. Every time our plane drops, the boxes rise to the level of my arm rests, float for a moment as if weightless, and then crash back down to the floor as the plane recovers. I know only too well: without whisky my mission is wasted. No alcohol, no morale.

Yet, the entire plane already reeks of alcohol. The situation is so absurd that, for once, I escape becoming airsick.

In the work camp we are greeted with some reticence and trepidation. But there are enough unbroken bottles to go around, much as in Western movies. I assure my countrymen that we, in Algiers, bear up daily with the much more dangerous situation of city guerrilla warfare. I also promise to help get them out in time if need be.

As I say that – not entirely convinced – I cannot help but anticipate the fate of the Algerian indigenous force – the Harkis – who guard this camp. They stand around, quiet, sober and pensive. Their confidence is based on faith and faith alone: Islam. The German workers' morale, however, needs alcoholic uplifting.

I found the solution

As Attaché to the German Consulate General in Algiers, I have witnessed terrible scenes of crime and terror during the past nine months. Hardly a night has passed without plastic explosions – some nights up to a hundred or more. Month after month, in Algiers alone, about 1,000 people have been gunned down, mostly at very short range. The National Liberation Front (FLN) fights France in order to make Algeria an independent State.

The Pieds Noirs, the French and Spanish settlers of colonial Algeria, fight Paris as well, but to maintain the country under French sovereignty. And it is their secret army, the *Organisation Armée Secrète* (OAS), that sends ignited gasoline trucks into Algerian quarters and hunts Algerian men as if they were rabbits. From my apartment in El-Biar, I see what is left of a mountain village after it has been attacked with napalm by French forces. When searching for German patients in the Mustapha Hospital, I see new victims rushed in every twenty minutes, invariably shot in the head, in most cases from behind.

An armistice is currently being observed between France and the FLN, and a date for independence has been set. Consequently, the OAS – with many deserted German legionaries in its ranks – is now frantically trying to provoke the Algerians through increased terror to lash back, thus violating their armistice with France and postponing independence, perhaps indefinitely.

With this insidious design, OAS commandos have begun to liquidate the young Algerian intelligentsia at universities, and Algerian women – so far taboo – are being killed as they go shopping.

When our neighbour's children came home wide-eyed the other day, much disturbed by bestialities they had seen committed on Algerians, their mother consoled them, saying, "C'était seulement des Arabes!" Only Arabs…

Throughout that period, always armed with a cocked 7.65 mm Walther PK pistol, I repeatedly searched for the secret that allowed those disciplined Algerians to take in their stride so much disdain, abuse, and punishment. At last I found the solution, while re-reading the Qur'ān. Verse 153 of *Sūrah al-Baqarah* says: "O you who have attained to faith! Seek aid in steadfast patience and prayer: for, behold, God is with those who are patient in adversity."

How Muslims tick

For the last two years, I have been responsible, at my level within the Political Division of the Foreign Office, for German relations with India, Pakistan, Ceylon, Nepal, Bhutan and Sikkim.

No matter how often I deal with Hindu or Buddhist Indians or Ceylonese, I cannot reliably anticipate their reactions. On the other hand, I seem to know precisely how Pakistani or Muslim Indians, even from Bangladesh, "tick". Their reactions are predictable. This phenomenon is not due to any mystical ties between Indo-Germanic people. There is a more rational explanation: Muslims adhere to a religion which, like ours, is based on a book that lends itself to legal inquiry. They, too, are "People of the Book" (*ahl al-kitāb*).

Prof. Muhammad Hamidullah, a polyglot Indian Muslim scholar, corroborated this conclusion when he revealed in 1941 that the constitution of the Federation of Madinah, promulgated by Muḥammad in the first year of the Hijrah, was the first written constitution in the history of statehood.

Thanks to Ibn Isḥāq, this astonishing document of fifty-two articles has come down to us intact. It deals with the social and economic integration of the Makkan immigrants; the legal relationships between this federated agglomeration's

Jewish and Arab tribes; rules for mutual assistance; coalition warfare; arbitration; and the right to grant asylum (M. Hamidullah, *The First Written Constitution in the World*, 3rd ed., Lahore 1975).

With such a background, it would indeed be surprising if legally trained Western and Muslim diplomats would not immediately find common ground.

Love for a buck

Hong Kong, 16 June 1971

During our long flight to Tokyo and Kyoto to participate in consultations between the German and the Japanese foreign policy planning staffs, I stop over with my boss, Dr. Dirk Oncken, in Hong Kong.

Flying high above Vietnam, we had been able to watch air attacks against the clearly visible Ho Chi Min trail while, with a touch of the surreal, our Air France stewardess served us an *haute cuisine* meal prepared by the Ritz. At this juncture, the British Crown colony is a typical base for troops behind the front, a "recreation area". Somebody seems to have called out loud and clear: "Prostitutes of all countries, here unite!"

As a Western tourist, one virtually has to fight off these girls when walking downtown, as if they were mosquitoes. It is especially heartbreaking when a Chinese teenager clings to me with the desperate plea: "One dollar only, Sir!" In order to earn more, these girls probably have to offer a bit more than usual and engage in outright perversions, like some of the especially sadistic Chinese forms of sodomy.

At any rate, as it was, the US Forces – even in those pre-AIDS days – suffered as many casualties from venereal diseases as they did in the real war.

Whenever sexual decadence leads to problems for the masses, Christian reactions are predictable. Initially, there is a wagging of the moral finger; some even see homosexuals and drug addicts as victims of the well-deserved revenge of God. Later on, in view of medially more plausible explanations, such metaphysical and therefore "irrational" analyses are rejected. Instead, Christians are reminded that they should show sympathy for those of their neighbours who brought misery upon themselves.

Muslims see matters somewhat more soberly. They know that God's rules for human conduct are made not for Him but for man. Whether people abide by these "moral" or "ethical" norms or not is entirely without consequences for Him. As 'Abd al-Qādir Jīlānī put it and Ibn 'Arabī endorsed it: "God is rich without His creation." If they respect these norms, human beings do themselves a favour; and if they do not respect them, they harm themselves. There is no more to it than that.

Take a drunken driver who runs into a tree, or a bisexual male who acquires AIDS and passes it on to his unsuspecting wife: the mechanics are the same. They are not "punishments" but the sheer "natural" consequences of living in contradiction with, and in opposition to, the innate order of the reality of which we are a part.

From this perspective it is most appropriate that the Islamic code of behaviour – the *Sharī'ah* – is called "road". To stay on that road is the Muslim's most frequently reiterated request: whenever they recite the opening *sūrah* of the Qur'ān, the *Fātiḥah*, they pray to be guided on the "straight path".

In Bishop Arius' tracks

Vienna, 2 November 1974

Shortly after his strenuous and dangerous pilgrimage to
Madinah and Makkah in 1853, the British explorer, Sir
Richard Burton (1821–1890), gave a photographically accurate
account of his adventure in his *Personal Narrative of a Pilgrimage
to Al-Medinah & Meccah*. It is an irreplaceable source of
information on the Hijaz region.

Quite a few eyebrows were raised in the Victorian society
of the day because Burton had apparently lied a bit too much
in pretending to be a Muslim. Other critics accused him of the
opposite: had Burton not been a bit too sincere in acting like a
Muslim? Indeed, he had penetrated the faith, history, language,
and culture of Islam to an unprecedented degree.

Today, it seems that Burton had become not only a Muslim
but even a sufi in the *ṭarīqah* (order) of 'Abd al-Qādir Jīlānī – a
fact to which the author could not more than allude in the
third edition of his book in 1879. At that time, in the spirit of
mystical Unitarianism, Burton pointed out that the Muslims
(who also revered Abraham) – as "heterodox Christians, namely
followers of Arianism" – were closer to the teachings of Jesus
than Christians who followed the interpretations given later
by St. Paul and Bishop Athanasius. Muslims were at any rate
more enlightened, more tolerant, and more brotherly than most
Christians.

Of course, Burton found it impossible to overcome the typical defensive mechanism with which Westerners fend off facts about Islam that do not fit their favourite prejudices. This psychological blockage of perception functions almost as well today as it did during the Crusades, regardless of the recent shift of the Vatican's position towards this sister religion.

Tolerance institutionalized

Sofia, 26 July 1976

Returning from the 8th International Ballet Competition in Varna on the Bulgarian Black Sea cost – the unofficial Olympics of the world of dance – I discover, in Sofia, a little church lying beneath street level, as if it had sunk into a ditch. This strange building, the St. Petra Samarjinska, is a major attraction of the Bulgarian capital. It was constructed when the country formed part of the Ottoman Empire. My guide interprets this odd positioning of a church as evidence of Muslim discrimination against a Christian minority. I see it from another angle.

I knew, after all, that the Spanish Christians, after the Reconquista, had brutally destroyed each and every mosque – from Malaga to Granada, and from Seville to Toledo. The magnificent building in Cordoba was saved, in a mutilated state, only because it could be turned into a cathedral. As late as in the 19th century, the Great Mosque of Algiers suffered the same fate.

I also knew that it was useless to search for any of the hundreds of mosques that once existed in Serbia and Greece under Turkish rule. In Belgrade, only one tiny mosque, that has no architectural interest, has been saved from being razed with all the others.

What a remarkable contrast: Muslim conquerors not only allowed the Christian cult to continue in existing churches, but they even permitted additional churches to be built under Islamic rule. How else would today's tourists be able to marvel at jewels such as the famous Byzantine Chora Church (Kariye Cami) and the Greek-Orthodox and Armenian cathedrals in Istanbul? If Christian intolerance had been the Islamic model, what would be left today of the Serbian cloisters and churches on Lake Ohrid, of Gracanica, Decani, Sopocani, Pec and Studenica, and of the majestic Hagia Sophia in Istanbul?

The marked difference between Christian intolerance and Muslim tolerance is based on the Qur'ān's strict command to tolerate the faithful of other "people of the Book" (*ahl al-kitāb*), which was developed into a detailed code of law protecting both minorities and foreigners. Verse 256 of *Sūrah al-Baqarah* clearly states: "There shall be no coercion in matters of faith." Religious pluralism is sanctioned in *Sūrah* 5, verse 48, as a healthy competition among the pious before their Lord. *Sūrah* 42, verse 8 is equally explicit: "Had God so willed, He could surely have made them all one single community..." Such tolerance will be better understood when one realizes that Muslims view Jesus as the greatest of all prophets in the Jewish tradition. "We gave thee (O Muḥammad) insight through revelation – as well as that which We had enjoined upon Abraham, Moses, and Jesus..." (42:13)

Under the liberal Islamic statutes governing minority rights and privileges, Christians were allowed to organize their own community and to profess their religion in their churches. Long before the notion of "conscientious objection" arose, non-Muslims were exempted from military service by paying a fairly assessed tax instead (*jizyah*). Like the Jewish communities under Christian rule, protected subjects (*dhimmī*) in Islamic countries also had to wear specific clothing. They could not embark on a governmental or military career, but they retained the possibility of competing in the market and succeeding in the arts. They were even allowed to produce and consume pork and wine. Moreover, according to Islamic law *(fiqh)* – as under Roman law – contracts were to be kept without regard to the partner's denomination.

Alas, not in theory but in practice, the infamous Crusades often led to a considerable deterioration of the fate of Christians under Muslim rule. As a result, in the high Middle Ages, non-Muslims were not allowed to build churches taller than the mosques around them – hence the curious lowering of St. Petra Samarjinska. Scholars adhering to the Shāfi'ī school of *fiqh* even forbade church-bell ringing.

However, how much does such discrimination weigh in view of the fact that Christian rulers not only outlawed the *muezzin*'s call for prayer but Islam as such?

Fasting with a purpose

Belgrade, Ramaḍān 1977

My gardener, an Albanian from Serbia's Kosovo region in south-east Yugoslavia, is as lean as a rake, seems to have the nine lives of a cat, and is a devout Muslim. As if to honour his peculiar name – Ramadani Ramadan – he correctly fasts during the entire lunar month of Ramaḍān without in the least neglecting any of his chores. After interrupting his fasting with a light meal at the right moment of the evening – *ifṭār* – he walks three miles to Belgrade's only mosque, near the Kalemegdan park, in order to say his night prayers (*'ishā'* and *tarāwīḥ*) in the company of fellow Albanians and brethren from Sarajevo, Mostar, or other towns in the two Muslim republics of Communist Yugoslavia: Bosnia and Herzegovina.

Occasionally, we invite Ramadani to have the post-*ifṭār* meal with us. It is our only chance, since he would even refuse to have a cup of coffee with us in the morning – right from the moment he was able to distinguish a white thread from a black one in the light of dawn.

With similar insistence I had recently seen a Muslim passenger observe fasting during a JAT-flight to Istanbul. Checking his watch from time to time, he did not touch his meal – defending it, however, against being cleared away by the stewardess – until *ifṭār*, the right moment for breaking his fast, had arrived.

It would not matter when the fast exactly starts and terminates if the purpose of the exercise was merely to lose weight, put the body through a cleansing cure, show solidarity with the hungry in Africa, or steel one's discipline through mental fitness training. All these effects are merely spin-offs, windfall gains. Primarily, a Muslim abides by the rules of Ramaḍān because they have been laid down for him, the slave, by his Lord.

Without revelation, blind

Belgrade, 28 March 1978

I usually read two books in alternation, recovering from one difficult text by switching to another. Currently, I am practising this method with classics from Islamic philosophy of the 10–13th centuries, such as Ibn Rushd's *Tahāfut al-Tahāfut* (The Incoherence of the Incoherence) in translation by Simon Van den Bergh (London 1969).

As was customary in learned Western disputation until and during the 19th century, Averroes deals disdainfully, even abusively with his opponent, the eminent Abū Hāmid al-Ghazālī. Paragraph by paragraph Ibn Rushd quotes almost the complete text of al-Ghazālī's *Tahāfut al-Falāsifa* (The Incoherence of Philosophy), only to add, paragraph for paragraph, his refutation, introduced by a proud: "I, however, say..."

The Islamic philosophers of the early Middle Ages were caught in the very web of questions first spun by their Greek masters. Consequently, they also followed closely the footsteps of Plato, Aristotle, Plotinus, and Proclus. Like these, the Persian and Arab philosophers reduced their inquiry to questions concerning the eternity (or createdness) of the universe; the relationship between the existing and the potential; the nature of the soul, etc. However, these Muslim thinkers were most fascinated by cosmology: whether God, the Immovable, could be the Prime Mover? Why the celestial bodies orbited as they did and not in reverse? How many angels existed?

The most burning philosophical question of our age – the "why" or significance of our existence – was barely touched upon. They only came close to it when wondering whether God had created the world for Himself. Had these pious philosophers, charmed by that snake, Aristotle, fixed their gaze exclusively on the philosophic past? Or had they understood that is was fruitless, if not blasphemous, to engage in motivational research, with God on the couch?

Many ingeniously intelligent publications by Muslim thinkers have been preserved, written by intellectual giants such as al-Fārābī, al-Rāzī, al-Kindī, Ibn ʿArabī, Ibn Sīnā (Avicenna), and those already mentioned. Yet what impresses us most today is the sad realization that intelligent reasoning, when applied to questions of metaphysics, only leads to absurd speculations. These early philosophers have indeed proven one thing: that we cannot, through applying human logic, gain any reliable insight into the reality of the unseen. If God knows no past and no future, if His mode of existence is His eternal presence, and if He exists outside the confines of time and space, what can we know of Him thanks to intellectual (or indeed irrational) inquiry?

Against the riddle of our existence, even sensually perceivable reality – the things we can smell, touch and see – remains mysterious. In other words: without revelation, we are blind.

A weighty mouthful of water

As a try-out, we decided this year to observe the fast exactly as it is prescribed to Muslims. However, in contrast to a custom widespread in Islamic countries, we do not attempt to recoup during the night – at the expense of sleep – what had been foregone as nourishment during the day. (Would it have been in keeping with the spirit of the injunction against eating meat on Fridays if Catholics had had seafood orgies on those days?) It is at any rate important to make oneself drink as much liquid as possible before resuming the fast. (At least as a natural water reservoir, man cannot be compared with the camel.)

The first two days of fasting are the toughest: days of constant headache. It is therefore advisable to continue fasting even when the rules would permit an interruption, as during days of travel.

During the day, one must try to exploit to the maximum one's natural "ups" provided by biological curves. For that purpose, I divide my work into jobs that "must", "should" or "could" be done, and tackle the "must" tasks when my blood pressure reaches its natural peaks – in the late morning and in the middle of the afternoon. I also take great care not to jeopardize the lives of others (and my own) in traffic as a result of low blood sugar or tension. After all, the risks of causing lethal accidents through negligence and absent-mindedness have grown a thousand fold since the 7th century.

When fasting in Yugoslavia, one is constantly reminded of being an outsider. For instance, one must reject the otherwise welcome practice of being served Turkish coffee, juice and water in the Foreign Ministry in Kneza Milosa. However, when politely refusing such hospitality during Ramaḍān, I detect some understanding and even respect, if only because this supposedly atheistic country still houses about one million Muslim citizens.

After a week of fasting – no less than eighteen hours a day when Ramaḍān falls in the summer period – one reaches a point where economizing one's movements and speech becomes natural. I find myself moving slower, speaking only if necessary, and watching the haste and waste around me with detached contemplation, gaining everyday in independence and even, perhaps, in wisdom. When starting to eat in the evening, even the traditional initial olive followed by a mouthful of water, turns into a weighty ceremony. Like a thirsty plant just watered, a human body, too, can be quickly invigorated by so little. One now cherishes light, vegetarian food.

Day by day, one's morale seems to grow, as does one's confidence in setting priorities right. In the last analysis, is this fasting not primarily meant to develop immunity against the temptation called *shirk*: the risk of deifying what is entirely unessential in one's life?

Muscle aches, and a new morale

Edirne, 12 July 1978

Sinan, who was Sultan Süleyman the Magnificent's chief architect since 1539, crowned his life's achievements with the Selimiye Mosque in Edirne, built between 1567 and 1574.

Yet, few visitors know that he contrived three independent staircases within the single thin minaret. These wind themselves around each other without ever merging, except at a common entry and exit.

The mosque attendant made an exception when allowing me to ascend. But what a strain! Mostly in the dark, scaring bats and birds (and being, in turn, scared by them), I slowly moved ahead in a deeply crouched position, always advancing with the same leg. No other way in this narrow spiral confine. Soon my knees started trembling. But I could not contemplate changing direction since I could not turn. A critical situation, and one of high symbolism: I do not know when this climb will end but I know it will. I chose one direction, and this decision is irreversible.

When I finally returned, dirty, exhausted and somewhat troubled, I had gained enormously: a charlie-horse and a new morale!

Ballet competition –
theological competition

Belgrade, 26 January 1979

In my capacities as junior barrister, ballet critic, and executive secretary of the Munich Ballet Club, I used to organize annual dance matinees at the Gärtnerplatz Theatre. The programme was always based on individual contributions, uncensored, offered by private ballet schools. My real (but disguised) intention was to show naïve parents and dance students that there was a wide qualitative difference between the ballet schools, some of which were excellent, some miserable. My hope was that in competition with the former, the latter would eliminate themselves.

Perhaps Gerhard Szczesny secretly pursued the same scheme when publishing the results of an academic opinion poll among theologians from the Catholic, Protestant, Buddhist, Islamic, and Jewish faiths (*Die Antwort der Religionen*, Reinbek 1971, 1st ed. 1964). Whatever the editor's purpose, it is painful to read the vague, elliptical, belaboured answers given by the two Christian representatives, particularly when contrasted with the short, precise and sober replies given by Muhammad Asad for Islam and Kurt Wilhelm for Judaism.

The Protestant professor, Ernst Wolf, manages to fill several pages discussing the relationship between sensual and non-sensual reality, without feeling the need to refer, even once, to God.

And just witness how the Catholic professor, Johann Baptist Metz, indulges in verbosity: "Since this revelation through Jesus Christ is believed as the unique event of salvation in which man's existential question found its historically unsurpassable answer once and for all, this answer must remain authentic, present as a norm, and accessible for humanity throughout its history, and exactly this has become possible through the 'Sacred Scriptures', notwithstanding that this concretization in writing of the event of revelation was realized within a humanity which already possessed script as a medium of binding historical tradition." Wow!

Muhammad Asad, in contrast, crisply formulates the following: "Islam does not view reality dualistically… One therefore cannot contrast 'another reality' with 'our reality' but only speak of perceivable and non-perceivable aspects of one and the same totality." And: "Natural science alone is incapable of revealing all aspects of reality … In order to give us the necessary guidance which science cannot provide, God reveals to us in a way described as revelation, which God grants to certain particularly receptive personalities called prophets." Full stop.

Kismet is no excuse

Bonn, 27 February 1980

Muhammad Asad's enchanting biography, *The Road to Macca* (Frankfurt 1955), taught me that Oriental fatalism, well understood, is an attitude not toward the future, but toward the past. Accepting fate (*kismet*) is no excuse for twiddling thumbs. It simply means seeing God's will behind all that has happened, whether we like it or not.

Equally important for me was Asad's assessment that the duality of being, or rather the hostility against man's "carnal" self, which St. Paul carried into the Christian church, deprives man of his dignity as a perfect entity. As a result, Manichaeism was given a new lease on life in Christian disguise, separating even today the so-called "sacred" from the so-called "profane" in a way totally foreign to the holistic Muslim viewpoint.

Asad also draws one's attention to the often overlooked fact that Muḥammad revolutionized the value system of Arab society when he replaced the all-important tribal bonds (the nationalisms of the day) with the entirely new political concept of a "community" – his *ummah* – based solely on religious solidarity. Equally subversive were his instructions for prayer. To humbly throw themselves down in prostration before God must have gone against the very grain of those dignified, proud Bedouin Quraysh.

Dervish entertainment

Konya, 13 July 1980

From our hotel, we enjoy a fantastic view of the green dome built over the tomb of the Mawlānā, Jalāluddīn Rūmī; it is an exact copy of the one over the Prophet's mosque in Madinah. The religious order that was inspired by Rūmī, known as the "whirling dervishes" (*mevleviye tariqah*), survived being outlawed by Atatürk on 13 December 1925 about as well as the Jesuit order survived the Papal ban of 1773 for forty-one years.

Today's dervishes are presented as an entertaining folkloric show. However, the audience quickly discovers that it is participating in a practice that flowers on the fringes of Islam. It is immediately obvious that the dervishes' constant rotating motion is not a rare or strange dance, but a vehicle for religious contemplation.

My teacher on the ensemble's characteristic bamboo flute (*ney*) is an enthusiastic dervish himself. He tries to steer me towards studying, with priority, not the Qur'ān but his master's monumental literary *oeuvre*, the *Mesnevi* – an enormous collection of rich, mystically inspired religious poetry.

My *neysen* cherishes Rūmī's ecstatic, universal love lyrics because they seem to bridge all dogmatic differences. Indeed, these *mevlevi* lead their followers toward an optimistic unitarianism with Islamic colouring and pantheistic shadings. Is this what is meant by *ṭarīqah*, the "path"?

St. Paul, the Heretic

One cannot expect a reply if one asks how tall Jesus was; which colour he liked best; whether he had been fond of honey or garlic; or which shoe he put on first in the morning. To be sure, these are all rather banal aspects of an important person's life. But the point can be made: we know all of these and other details about the Prophet Muḥammad. From the Gospels, on the other hand, Jesus merely emerges as a legendary figure with vague contours. Some attribute this difference to the difficulty of documenting the life of a person who lived 600 years before Muḥammad.

There is a better explanation: the numerous, painstakingly collected and sifted accounts (aḥādīth) of the beginnings of Islam were given exclusively by trustworthy eyewitnesses and have been handed down to us in prestigious ḥadīth-collections. The Gospels, on the other hand, are to a large extent late reconstructions, frequently based on hearsay only. We hardly ever hear Jesus speak himself. Rather, we read later interpretations of what he meant to say.

As the New Testament is not a primary but secondary source, it by no means ranks with the Qur'ān. It may be better compared with an unsound collection of suspect aḥādīth. To give the most disturbing example: if the principles of Islamic research had been applied, all the letters of St. Paul would have been

36

eliminated from the New Testament because he had never seen, met, or spoken with Jesus.

Considering the pervasive influence that St. Paul's interpretation of the events surrounding Jesus had on the ideological development of Christendom, today's Christians (in contrast to the early Jewish Christians) might as well call themselves "Paulians". Truly, the Christian heresy – the reinterpretation of Jesus as God, the postulation of "Trinity", and the demonization of "the flesh" – began with Paul.

Business morals

Window-shopping in Istanbul's covered Bazar (Kapalı Çarşı), we stop for a moment in front of an unattended souvenir shop. Immediately, the owner of the adjacent shop offers to sell us items from his neighbour's display. No attempt to lure us over to his own souvenir shop or to generate business for himself.

Somewhere else, we pay fully in advance for a leather jacket to be made to order and delivered to Germany. We will receive it even though we never met the merchant before and probably will never meet him again either.

Later on, my wife asks a jeweller to assess the value of an impeccable diamond. For half an hour, he disappears with it to consult a friend more expert than himself. We are not nervous since we are certain to receive this diamond back, and no other.

How can such business ethics – merchants practising altruism instead of cut-throat competition – be explained? Is it due to the transparency of the bazar market, or a legacy of the high moral standards of the former guilt system? Does it result from a fatalistic approach to economic enterprise? Is it the fruit of the feeling of brotherhood in action?

These Islamic business morals are real and make it difficult to describe the economic system of Islam as an institutional alternative. There is no scarcity of literature on the subject (mainly on interest-free banking), but there is not a single live model of a functioning, purely Islamic economy. One of the main reasons for this is the absence of a clear-cut, comprehensive Islamic business code. As is true of the Basic Law of the Federal Republic of Germany and of the Constitution of the United States of America, the Qur'ān and the *Sunnah* mainly provide guidelines for the general framework of a market economy based on private property and social responsibility. The more specific rules are mainly limited to the fields of contracts and taxation, and are characterized by the proscription of pure interest payments, usury, and business deals with an element of gambling (such as speculation in commodities involving future goods).

The essence of the Islamic conduct of business must therefore be found in the relevant moral ordinances of the Qur'ān. It is no different from the foundations of a Christian economy. In fact, Islam can bring about a reform of business habits only – if at all – through a reform of man. What counts is not the system but the economic mentality and ethics of socially responsible Muslim producers and consumers, contractors and bankers.

Three times, not four

Istanbul, 29 July 1980

It is terribly hot as we battle our way through traffic in steamy Istanbul, using *dolmuş*, buses, and our aching feet in order to visit some friends who cannot be reached by telephone.

Zekiye, my mother-in-law, rings the doorbell once, twice, and – after a pause – a third time. No response. Without further ado, she turns away, preventing me from ringing a fourth time because "that just isn't done". In reacting this way, she was hardly conscious of observing a rule established by the Prophet; she acted as was customary in the Islamic world. Yet her reaction can be traced back to an incident recorded among rules of etiquette in the 74th Book of al-Bukhārī's famous *ḥadīth*-collection (*Ṣaḥīḥ al-Bukhārī*).

According to *ḥadīth* No. 261 reported by Anas, Muḥammad, when seeking admission, never announced his wish by greeting more than three times. If the door remained closed, he rightly assumed that people were either absent or unwilling to receive.

This is only one of many examples of how the behaviour of the Prophet of Islam became a natural way of life for an entire people. The more I study the vast collections of *aḥādīth* (particularly those assembled and verified by al-Bukhārī and Muslim), the more my sociologically trained eyes open. What I discern is Islam as a culture.

The Road to Macca

We are close enough to the end of the 20th century to be able to affirm that nobody during the last one hundred years has contributed more to the explanation and propagation of Islam in the West than the Austrian Muhammad Asad (formerly Leopold Weiss, of Jewish descent). His impact is not only due to the respect paid to his deep wisdom and learning, but also to his moral qualifications.

Born in 1900, Asad lived an adventurous life, which provided him with many opportunities to show and use his many talents. Aged 14, he ran away from home to join the Austrian army and fight in World War I. At 19, he worked as Dr. Murnau's assistant, and later for Max Reinhardt – both giants of early movie making.

By the age of 22, he had already become the Near East correspondent for Germany's most prestigious newspaper, the *Frankfurter Zeitung*. Subsequently, having embraced Islam in 1926, he became a friend of both King Ibn Sa'ūd and Muhammad Iqbal.

The end of World War II saw him in India. And when Pakistan was founded, he became Under Secretary of State for Near Eastern Affairs in the Foreign Ministry of this new State, which later was to send him to New York as its Permanent Representative to the United Nations.

These are but some of the more notable roles he filled in an altogether remarkable life, which integrated thought and action, philosophy and religion, aesthetics and politics in a genuinely Islamic fashion. Asad, a Renaissance man *à la* Islam!

All his books have now become classics in their own right. With *Islam at the Crossroads* (1934), Asad helped to restore dignity and cultural self-assurance to an apologetic Islamic world that had lost all self-confidence under the onslaught of Western technological supremacy. Writing more than fifty years ago in Delhi, Asad predicted the following with astonishing far-sightedness: "It may be… that the growing social and economic unrest, and possibly a new series of world wars of hitherto unknown dimensions and scientific terrors will lead the materialistic self-deceit of Western civilization in such a gruesome way *ad absurdum*, that its people will begin once more, in humility and earnest, to search after spiritual truths: and then a successful preaching of Islam in the West might become possible."

His brilliantly written autobiography, *The Road to Macca* (1954) is a moving document of his conversion to Islam. In his *Principles of State and Government*, Asad admits, without hesitation, that there has not been a truly Islamic State after Abū Bakr, 'Umar, 'Uthmān, and 'Alī – the first four caliphs who reigned from Madinah. He also affirms that the Qur'ān and the *Sunnah* contain only a few precise guidelines for the organization of an Islamic State and society. His conclusions are far-reaching:

1. the body of Islamic law, as it developed over eight centuries, is much vaster than its binding core (the *Sharī'ah*);
2. within the framework of a constitution (and legislation) reflecting this core, an Islamic State could show many

features typical of a parliamentary democracy and the rule of law, including the American institutions of president and supreme court;

3. a re-awakening of Islam is consequently not necessarily a re-establishment of an Islamic theocracy.

Asad did his homework in Madinah where, during several decades, he translated and annotated the initial part of al-Bukhārī's *ḥadīth*-collection (*Ṣaḥīḥ al-Bukhārī: the Early Years of Islam*, 1938), and the entire Qur'ān (*The Message of the Qur'ān*, 1980). This ingenious translation into Shakespearean English was a literary, scientific and historical event. For his commentary on the Qur'ān, Asad is indebted to the great Egyptian reformer and Qur'ān commentator, Shaykh Muḥammad 'Abduh (also author of the famous *Risālat al-Tawḥīd,* 1897). Indeed, like him, Asad always looked out for the most rational and most direct explanation, applying the latest insights of linguistics and natural science, and showing no false reverence for pious practices and legends that had taken over the living body of Islam to a point of inhibiting rational discourse.

That this great man, in defence of his spiritual and moral integrity, chose to move again, at over 80 years of age, from Madinah to Tangiers, and from there to Portugal and Spain, demonstrates to all that Muhammad Asad remains true to himself: critical, alert, alive.

Muslim emancipation

Bonn, 25 August 1980

The idea that sacrificing a man, woman or animal can buy forgiveness is as old (and as heathen) as can be. It is also a notion that definitely precedes the recognition of God as the "Benevolent and Merciful".When Christian dogmatists justified the crucifixion of Jesus as a "necessary sacrificial death", they continued to argue within the logic of this heathen cult of sacrifice. In order to be able (!) to forgive, God needs (!) His Self-sacrifice? Who, may I ask, has bound God by defining such needs and setting down such a condition? Is such thinking not sheer blasphemy?

The image of God presented to us in the Qur'ān, even in such "Christian" *sūrahs* and verses as *Sūrah al-Fātiḥah* and the Verse of the Throne (2:255), is less humanized, and much more sublime than the average Christian's concept of God. It is all the more remarkable that the Qur'ān does not admit any intercession in the relationship between the individual and his God. "Who is there that could intercede with Him, unless it be by His leave?" (2:255). No caliph, no *imām*, no saint, can intervene for a third person (in the Christian sense of "mediator").

In other words, as early as the 7th century AD, the Muslims were released from the tutelage implied in the administration of sacraments, and were thrown into an unmitigated, direct, existentialist relationship with God – a relationship that is more becoming for modern man, for a grown-up man.

The seal of all prophets

Bonn, 27 August 1980

The concept of a "One-and-Only God" inevitably had to develop in the course of man's intellectual maturation. Polytheism had to transform itself into a hierarchy of gods, if only because each conqueror superimposed his tribal god(s) over those of the subdued. It was a decisive stage in the process towards the recognition of the highest ranking of the gods.

The Jewish breakthrough to monotheism was flawed because it continued to view Jehovah as a tribal god.

Jesus corrected this misconception. But the message of this "son of God" became warped when his followers took his kinship with God literally.

Another prophet had to come who would preach the sublime One-and-Only God for all. This final breakthrough is the monumental contribution of Islam to the spiritual development of mankind. The fact that perfection and truth cannot be improved upon makes Muḥammad the "seal of all prophets".

Islam *à la carte?*

As a former agnostic adept of Ludwig Wittgenstein one is tempted to approach Islam selectively. In particular, one tries to distinguish in the Qur'ān between eternally valid theological statements and outdated rules for the conduct of daily life. One seeks to be reasonable, avoiding exaggeration, and therefore drops, as overruled by the passage of time, the "antiquated" aspects of the Book.

Praying five times a day? Fasting for a whole month? Foregoing alcohol and interest payments? Not bad, perhaps, but simply no longer practisable in a modern technological society.

As one responds in that way, one has begun to bowdlerize the Qur'ān, choosing from it *à la carte*, and engaging in selective submission to the will of God.

Converts to Islam are known to exude a quiet, secure sense of direction; they seem to be in joyful harmony with themselves and their environment. But how is one to experience what Islam can do unless one's submission is total?

Muslim in spite of myself

Bonn, 11 September 1980

For some time now, striving for ever more precision and brevity, I have tried to put on paper, in a systematic way, all philosophical truths which, in my view, can be ascertained beyond reasonable doubt. The result of this lifetime struggle with man's limited access to reality is to be an unconventional birthday gift for my son Alexander.[1]

In the course of this effort, it dawned on me that the typical attitude of an atheist is not an intelligent one; that man simply cannot escape a decision to believe; that the createdness of what exists around us is obvious; that Islam undoubtedly finds itself in the greatest harmony with overall reality. Thus I realize, not without shock, that step by step, in spite of myself and almost unconsciously, in feeling and thinking, I have grown into being a Muslim.

Only one last step remains to be taken: to formalize my conversion.

---

1. Now available as a publication of 16 pages only: *A philosophical approach to Islam* (3rd German edition, Munich 1997; English edition: Cologne 1983 ISBN 3–8217–0025–4).

Lā ilāha illallāh,
Muḥammad rasūlullāh

Bonn, 25 September 1980

My confession of faith, the *shahādah*, has been deposited with the Islamic Centre in Cologne: *"Lā ilāha illallāh, Muḥammad rasūlullāh"*. I chose Murad as my Islamic name.

As of today I am a Muslim.

I have arrived.

Why not quadruplicity?

Bonn, 26 September 1980

If a Holy Trinity can be imagined, why not a quadripartite godhead? If the "First Born", namely the "Emanation", is of the same nature as the Prime Cause, why does a second emanation not also participate in that nature? Could the notion of Trinity have developed if the Fathers of the Church had been unaware of the post-Platonic philosophers Plotinus and Proclus who, in their *Liber de causis*, distinguished between "Existence" (Father?), "Reason" (Holy Ghost?) and "Soul" (Son?) – a tetralogy of emanations as much Gnostic as Christian?

The whirling dervishes of Konya

Bonn, 9 October 1980

In Bonn's Beethoven Hall, the whirling dervishes of Konya are presented as if they were an exhibition dance ensemble. Consequently, many people in the audience expect an ecstatic whirling of Dionysian, if not orgiastic, dancers instead of the contemplative ecclesiastical ceremony they are about to see. The performers – disciplined urban, married monks – are the very opposite; they represent the ultimate in classical religious poetry and music of Turkey.

Their ceremony begins with a Persian song of praise by Jalāluddīn Rūmī, rendered by a blind *ḥāfiz*, Kani Karaca, with an imposing but entreating *basso profundo* voice. The *Mevlevi-* dervishes, dressed in their symbol-rich costumes, enter without a sound: their cone-shaped felt hats (*sikke*) represent tomb stones; their black kaftans evoke the darkness of the grave; and their white bolero jackets and skirts recall shrouds.

The dervishes first circumambulate three times with irregular, retarding steps. Whenever they pass their *shaykh* at his place of honour (post), they turn in order to bow mutually with the following dervish. They bend deeply when kissing the *shaykh*'s hand; he slightly bends and kisses their *sikke*.

Only then do the *Mevlevi* start to turn, initially holding their arms crossed with their hands on their shoulders. Soon, however, their arms unfold – the right palm reaching to the sky, the left one turned to the floor. (Everything comes from God, from above; and everything he receives, the dervish passes on lovingly to his fellow man.) The dervishes rotate serenely, at the same, even, effortless rhythm, whether staying on one spot, or moving. A ballet critic would identify their motion as turns to the left, *en dedans*, during a count of four – the preparation (change of feet) taking three parts and swinging around the right leg to complete the turn of the fourth part.

The dervishes continue this routine for an incredible 20–25 minutes, never showing any trace of sweat, dizziness, or shortness of breath. These mystics have been described sometimes as white butterflies, sometimes as planets circling a spiritual centre. No wonder, for who can watch them without becoming hypnotized by their quiet whirling in regular waves? One is now close to penetrating a highly refined physical method for inducing religious ecstasy in the name of Islam.

Their old *shaykh*, Selman Tüzün, due to his formidable authority, has an unusual stage presence. His own turning is delicate, slow motion, as if in a trance, yet with great visual impact. By now the audience realize, to the last man or woman, that this is not the familiar painful spectacle of an ageing dancer refusing retirement. What we are witnessing is ageless charisma based on asceticism.

The immunity of Islam

Bonn, 26 February 1981

When Muslims compare the risks posed by the Communist world with those posed by the West, many are more afraid of Western spiritual subversion than of being physically trampled by Communism. This results from their correct observation that neither the Soviet Union, nor even the Soviet tanks in Afghanistan, have so far succeeded in exterminating Islam.

It is not possible to critically damage Islam in the same way as Christianity, by arresting bishops and priests, preventing the administration of sacraments, or confiscating their holy books. Indeed, thousands of Soviet Muslims are *ḥāfiz* (know the Qur'ān by heart). Moreover, Muslims can pray, if need be individually, in any clean place, anywhere. This is one of the secrets of the resistance that Islam has demonstrated over considerable periods under totalitarian rule. It accounts for the astonishing fact that millions of Chinese Muslims survived Mao Tse-Tung and the Cultural Revolution, and that several hundred Spanish Muslim families not only survived the Reconquista but also the rule of Francisco Franco.

Alas, Islam is not equally immune to less open and less systematic missionary work: the insidious sapping of its strength, not by a particular Christian effort, but by the subtle and pervasive influence of Western technological civilization.

Western industrial society has a toxic effect on all religions, including its own, by propagating values based on purely materialistic assumptions. Utility thinking, maximization of profit, the fetish of constantly increasing productivity, the mythology of endless progress, the arrogance of natural scientists turned philosophers, and the rampant agnosticism and value-neutralism of the educated – the entire Western drive to "rationalize" every aspect of life is fundamentally inimical to religion. The technocratic society in which we, in the West, live, with its cult of the individual and its moral *laisser faire/ laisser passer* attitude, is indeed in danger of fully destroying the ethical foundations on which this very society grew: values and modes of behaviour rooted in our forefathers' faith in God.

Turkey is the prime example of this process in terms of de-Islamification. Atatürk viewed his compatriots' religion as a handicap for modernization because of Islam's allegedly backward orientation. In Turkish cities, Islam has in fact been buried beneath a cult of progress, prosperity, and "scientific" problem solving. This is at least true of the so-called educated members of the upper and middle classes in urban areas. They are more likely to worship science than their Creator.

Nevertheless, some of these enlightened products of secularized Turkey are fond of claiming: "I am not a practising Muslim, but deep in my heart I believe in Allah. This natural faith of mine is worth more than praying five times a day." It is common to hear such a statement from "Muslims" whose vague knowledge of their fathers' religion is limited to some, frequently curious and marginal, aspects orally transmitted to them by their grandmothers.

If Atatürk had not relegated religious instruction to the underground, educated Turks would probably understand that not even Islamic mystics ever perceived religion as a matter of the heart alone. These self-styled "modern" Muslims would perhaps recognize that Islam – submission to God – implies submission as well to His guidance, instructions and laws.

Against this background, it is ironic that a Turkish Agency of Religious Affairs nowadays frantically tries to curb the negative effects of having neglected Islam for so long, which was clearly detrimental to the nation's quest for identity in the modern age. State-trained and State-paid Turkish *imāms* and *hocas* (teachers) are now sent out as far as Germany with the belated and difficult task of gaining control of the large unofficial network of Qur'ānic schools, mosques, and Sufi congregations that sprang up among Turkish workers in reaction to Atatürk's secularization policy.

Muslim international law

The term "international law" implies worldwide recognition. However, the Law of Nations has always been valid only in as much as it has been honoured and observed "nationally". In recent times, we have had to learn again that there can be a special, regional international law even though this seems to amount to a *contradictio in adiecto.*

Regionalism in the Law of Nations is, in fact, not only a phenomenon of Latin America and the Communist world, where the sinister notion of "proletarian internationalism" culminated with the so-called Brezhnev Doctrine. Until the end of the Crimean War, the Islamic world did not participate either in the development of international law among the Christian nations.

As a matter of principle, even today this cannot be otherwise because the *Sharī'ah* denies both the concept of "natural" law and the possibility of peace treaties between Islamic and non-Islamic states. However, rather than nourishing the romantic notion of a Family of Nations, Islamic law emphasizes the difference between the Muslim in-group (*dār al-Islām*, the house of Islam) and the non-Muslim out-group (*dār al-ḥarb*, the house of war). Equally important is the fact that Islamic legal theory postulates that all Muslims form a singly unity – the *ummah* – and it therefore rejects the idea of a multitude of States.

Consequently, Islamic law, to this day, refuses to treat the intercourse between Muslim communities as inter-state relations.

As Hans Kruse (*Islamische Völkerrechtslehre*, 2nd ed., Bochum 1979) has demonstrated, Islamic jurisprudence nevertheless has been able to cope with the hard facts of international conflict.

Firstly, Islamic scholars — like their Western colleagues — have taught that contracts and treaties must be honoured regardless of the religion of the other party. It makes no practical difference that Muslim lawyers based this fundamental rule of *pacta sunt servanda* on a divine Qur'ānic command rather than on a norm of customary international law. What counts is that Muslims, in deference to domestic law, abide by international treaties (which are honoured by non-Muslims in deference to international law).

Secondly, Muslim jurists cleverly devised legal fictions enabling them to reconcile brutal reality with sophisticated legal theory. Thus they justified the (inadmissible) development of lasting peaceful relations between Muslim and non-Muslim states on the basis of a tacitly prolonged (permissible) armistice.

Haute couture scandal

Istanbul, 1 August 1981

Today is *'Īd al-Fiṭr*, the Islamic holiday celebrating the end of Ramaḍān. As it happens, it showed me three different faces of Islam. Early in the morning, I participated in the long prayers that separate the month of fasting from the celebration, for three days, of *Şeker Bayramı* (Feast of Sweets). The mosque in Teşvikiye was overflowing. Many of the faithful brought their own prayer rugs (*seccade*), but like most others in the courtyard in front of the mosque I prayed on a decent newspaper, today's morning edition.

At noon, we visited the Eyüp Sultan Mosque on the upper shores of the Golden Horn. Ever since this building was constructed over the grave of Ayyūb, Muḥammad's standard bearer, miraculously located during the Turkish siege of 1453, legends and customs have surrounded this mosque and its picturesque site.

This is the closest thing in Islam to a devotional Christian shrine. What else am I to make of the custom of drinking from four water fountains on the four corners of a fence that surrounds a tree in close vicinity to the mosque, first opening all taps, then closing them one by one? Lovers, parents, students, soldiers – whoever harbours intense wishes – here feeds 1,001 doves with a kilogram of Indian corn, reserving, however, a number of grains to be strewn after the desired event takes

57

place. Other visitors carry animals to be promptly sacrificed in the name of Allah from the nearby market to a kitchen for the destitute poor (an annex to the Eyüp Sultan Mosque).

And of course the crowd at Eyüp Sultan would not be typical without a large number of young *sünnetli*-boys dressed up as generals, admirals and princes. They will be circumcised the following day. (In this way boys are feted as their sisters will be when getting married.)

The Wahhābītes would certainly put a violent end to these folkloric and superstitious aspects of popular Islam. After all, they do not tolerate commercial turmoil and exploitation near the Prophet's Mosque, in the interest of decorum, much to the detriment of local colour and popular enjoyment.

In the evening, we attend a fashion show. One of the most attractive dresses, made of black silk crepe, is virtually a scandal for its silver design consists of Qur'ānic passages exotically written in Arabic. The graphic beauty of it attracts a lot of innocent applause from people who would be horrified if they could understand the writing. But one generation after Atatürk, Arabic script has become as foreign as Chinese to people who used to read Arabic and write their own language with Arabic script. Is this what is meant by "progress"?

Ibn Khaldūn, not Marx

Bonn, 28 April 1982

Those who still believe that it is in the nature of Islam to impede progress would do themselves a favour if they read *Al-Muqaddimah*, the introductory book of Ibn Khaldūn's monumental world history (*Kitāb al-'Ibar*) written in 1377 (translated into English by Franz Rosenthal, Princeton 1967). If Ibn Khaldūn, supreme judge (*qāḍī*) in Cairo, had produced no more than those 1400 introductory pages, he would have made intellectual history. As it is, 500 years before Karl Marx and Max Weber, he became the real father of both sociology and the philosophy of history, requiring history to be "more than just information".

His is the earliest known attempt to discover the laws that govern historical cycles, the rise and fall of civilizations, and to write history after submitting traditional source materials to an impartial, critical, even skeptical scrutiny. This approach led Ibn Khaldūn to study the interaction between climate and behaviour, and between urban specialization and cultural traits.

It was not Karl Marx but he who wrote that "profit is the value realized from human labour" and that "different conditions among people are the result of different ways in which they make their living." Long before Thomas Mann (*Buddenbrooks*), Ibn Khaldūn had already declared that

"prestige lasts, at best, four generations in one lineage."
Centuries ahead of Friedrich Nietzsche, he had announced
that "while a nation is savage, its royal authority extends
farther." Before Friedrich Hegel, Ibn Khaldūn had noted that
"dynasties have a natural life span like individuals." Before
Jean-Jacques Rousseau, he had stated that the relationship
between the governing and the governed is based on a (social)
contract (concluded with a handshake and an oath of
allegiance). Well in advance of the modern theory of
legitimacy, Ibn Khaldūn had argued (against the Shī'a sect)
that "only he who has gained superiority over a nation … is
able to handle its affairs (as caliph)". Anticipating David Hume,
he had stressed that "the way in which causes exercise their
influence upon things is unknown." Centuries before Carl
von Clausewitz, Ibn Khaldūn taught that "there is no certainty
of victory" since "victory in war comes from luck and chance."
Like Friedrich Schiller and Immanuel Kant, he too traced
aesthetic judgments on visual objects back to philosophical
categories, without overlooking the interplay of psychological
mechanisms. (He recognized, for instance, that man cannot
but perceive the human form as being perfectly harmonious.)

I am particularly attracted to Ibn Khaldūn's rational approach
to ontology and Sufism. As a student of al-Ash'arī, he denies
any possibility of metaphysical insights derived from man's
sensual perception and intellect. "The intellect, indeed is a
correct scale… However, the intellect should not be used to
weigh such matters as the Oneness of God, the other world,
the truth of prophecy, the real character of divine attributes…
One might compare it with a man who sees a scale in which
gold is being weighed, and wants to weigh mountains in it."
Can one put it better?

Addressing mysticism, Ibn Khaldūn suspects that Sufis
artificially seek to experience, before death, what they will

realize after death. His judgment is stern: "Whatever supernatural knowledge or activity is achieved by the Sufis is accidental." Among the adepts of Sufism, Ibn Khaldūn discovers "fools and imbeciles who are more like insane persons than like rational beings." He maintains that "all these ways of perceiving the supernatural are based upon no proof, and are not viable."

But let us not forget: Ibn Khaldūn was neither an exceptional genius, nor an aberration. He was the product of Islamic culture at its best.

Sunnī versus Shī'ī

Bonn, 19 May 1982

From the Iranian Embassy, I receive a German translation of the new constitution of the Islamic Republic. As in all of its official communications, the Embassy, instead of using the traditional formulae of politeness, "avails itself of the opportunity" to express its revolutionary wish that the oppressed may triumph over their oppressors. This Iranian Constitution sees itself as the basis for the continuation of the Islamic revolution at home and abroad and as a mandate to form one single religious world community.

Not since the Communist Manifesto was first published in 1848, has the world heard such things. Article 154 obliges the Iranian Republic to support the just struggle of the oppressed against their oppressors everywhere in the world. According to Article 5, in view of the concealment of the Shī'a sect's Twelfth Imām, leadership of this global effort is for the time being entrusted to the Ayatollah Khomeini.

While basically a legal instrument, this Constitution does not fail to register the desire that God may send the absent, veiled Imām at the earliest possible moment. As a result of the Tehran hostage drama in 1979 (when the staff of the United States Embassy was held captive with official state blessing), of the peculiarities of the long drawn-out war between Iraq and Iran, and of the suicidal attacks of Shī'ī commandos in Lebanon, the entire world, including the Muslim peoples, has been watching with growing fascination the phenomenon of contemporary Persia: the rise of a fundamentalist Shī'ī State, the first authentic event of this nature since the Fatimids governed Egypt one thousand years ago.

Most Muslims know the important role Persians played in and for Islam since its origin. Salmān, Muḥammad's financial counsellor, was Persian, and so were many of the greatest minds in the history of Islamic sciences and philosophy, from al-Fārābī and Ibn Sīnā, to al-Ghazālī and al-Zamakhsharī. Muslims are also aware of the unique fecundity, in terms of religious fantasy, that has characterized Persians and Persia throughout history. In fact, no other country has ever created or sheltered so many different religions: Sun and fire worshippers, Gnostics, Platonists, Zoroastrians, Mazdeans, Manichaeans, Parsis, Druzes, Nestorians, Ahl al-Ḥaqq, Yazīdī (with the defamatory name of "devil-worshippers"), Alevis, Babi (or Baha'is), Sevener and Twelver Shī'ī. And that is not all.

However, no matter how critical a Sunnī Muslim (in other words, a majority Muslim) is likely to be *vis-à-vis* the theology and practice of the Shī'a sect, he will never permit himself to declare that a Shī'ī is not Muslim. One authority alone is competent to pass such a verdict: God. And He alone knows best. Muḥammad said: "When a man calls his brother an unbeliever, the criticism returns upon himself." (Muslim, *Ṣaḥīḥ*, Book I.)

The conflicting views of majority Sunnī Islam and the Shī'a sect all find their roots in the political situation that developed shortly after the Prophet's death. In stark contrast to Sunnīs, the Shī'ī do not concede to all faithful equal access to a correct and full understanding of the entire Qur'ān. This, and by inference also the function of the *khalīfah*, are seen as privileges of Muḥammad's close blood-relatives and their descendants.

The implications of this elitist approach of an Islamic nobility, if not priesthood, are far-reaching. For instance, the Shī'ī reject as illegitimate the first three caliphs (who preceded Muḥammad's son-in-law, 'Alī) and the entire body of their decisions and traditions. Worse yet, the Shī'a sect's approach reduces the ideal of equality in Islam, its internationality and globality. Composure and soberness ("patience in adversity") – hallmarks of the Sunnī ideal – also stand in stark contrast to the Shī'a sect's revolutionary protest with its almost structural sullen anger, which finds its most extreme expression in public flagellation. It is difficult to see how Islam – described in the Qur'ān as a "religion of the middle path" – could ever become reconciled with such exaggeration.

Muslims are admonished to be realists. And if they are, they cannot overlook the fact that the Western perception of what is currently happening in the Islamic Republic of Iran severely limits the chances of Islam's acceptance in the West – at least as long as the Sunnī and Shī'ī are wrongly seen as identical.

Iran's tremendous urge to serve God provides us with a fascinating example of how – to use Max Weber's terminology – an ethics focusing on motivation (*Gesinnungsethik*) can be counter-productive in a world preferring an ethics focusing on the results of action (*Verantwortungsethik*).

The First Council of Nicaea

Iznik, 21 July 1982

Whether Christian or Muslim, whoever harbours any feeling for the fateful power of historical decisions is overwhelmed when visiting Iznik, the former city of Nicaea, which is situated not far from Istanbul. Shortly after the Crusaders had thoroughly sacked Christian Constantinople (1204), this dusty, sleepy town briefly served as the capital-in-exile of the Byzantine Empire. But more importantly, it was here, in 325, that the religious fate of mankind was sealed. And one can still locate the site where a majority of bishops, attending the first Council of Nicaea (19 June–25 August 325), rigorously adopted the original Nicene Creed, according to which God, the Father and Jesus are "consubstantial".

The opposite creed, held by Arius, priest of Alexandria (260–336), nevertheless remained the official position under Emperor Constantine the Great (337–361). Indeed, even after a second condemnation of Arianism in 381, the conviction that Jesus, while a divinely created man, was neither equal to nor co-eternal with the Father, continued strong, particularly among the Germanic tribes. However, this drama has been wiped out of Western Christian consciousness, and so too, the teachings of Nestorius, Patriarch of Constantinople (381–451), ever since his view – that God and Jesus co-exist separately in one person – was illegitimatized by the Council of Ephesus in 431.

It is nevertheless a fact that for the first 500 years of Christianity, it was possible to be a faithful Christian without accepting the thesis that Jesus was consubstantial with the Father. From the Islamic point of view, Arian and Nestorian Christians are, and always have been, nothing less than Muslims.

In fact, if in 325 a few bishops (roughly 125) had resisted the extremist thesis of the substantial identity of Jesus and God, there would be no fundamental theological difference between Jews, Christians, and Muslims. One cannot help shuddering when pondering the responsibility for the fate of mankind that those few bishops (lightly?) shouldered at Nicaea.

A church is not a mosque

Bursa, 22 July 1982

Bursa, the old Ottoman capital, simultaneously offers skiing (on the Ulu Dağ mountain) and swimming (in the Marmara Sea). But one of its oddest curiosities is the Ulu Cami (Great Mosque) situated right in the heart of town. Its interior walls are virtually a museum of Arabic calligraphy – an art driven to stylistic variety and perfection by the Turks.

Equally striking is a whispering water fountain inside the mosque that serves as a sort of municipal meeting place. Here, tired tourists rest after praying their obligatory two prayer units (*rak'ah*) of salutation; students, gently rocking their torsos, recite the Qur'ān; and other visitors perform their ritual ablutions (*ābdest*).

Near the prayer niche (*miḥrāb*), one always finds a few Muslims deeply absorbed in contemplation and the adoration of the Unseen. Others, nearby, take a short nap before the mid-afternoon prayer.

Western visitors who are accustomed to churches that are used solely for religious services (and are locked-up afterwards), may be puzzled by all this. They have yet to learn that a mosque, housing neither an altar nor a tabernacle (both surrounded with taboos), needs to be no more than a clean place where people may gather and pray. Once this is understood, they will readily grasp the significant integrating function of mosques as socio-political centres, often surrounded by kitchens, libraries, baths, schools or cemeteries.

Too good to be true?

Bonn, 19 September 1982

The Minister-Counsellor of the Saudi Arabian Embassy receives me while my request for a pilgrim visa is being processed. However, in contrast to other foreign diplomats these days, he does not ask me questions about NATO's decision to station medium-range nuclear missiles in Europe. Rather, his burning interest focuses on a very different problem: what will be the roles of Jesus and Muḥammad, and their mutual relationship, shortly before and after the Final Judgment? And my host knows all there is to know from *ḥadīth*-literature about this rather speculative topic.

What fascinates me at this juncture is the astonishing fact that, here in the 20th century, there is a country whose diplomats may give religious issues priority over political ones.

Too good to be true?

Alcohol-nicotine-pork society

LH 624, 18 December 1982

As we approach Jeddah on our Lufthansa flight from Frankfurt, most German passengers – mainly women and children carrying Christmas trees as cabin baggage – frantically order, and consume, as much whisky and gin as possible before landing. After all, with touchdown, the terrible alcohol-free sojourn in their husbands, or fathers' construction camps will begin.

What a blatant demonstration of the sad fact that we, in the West, are living in a self-destructive alcohol-laden environment, or better, in an alcohol-nicotine-pork society. It is an experience that makes me wish I had booked this flight with a "dry" airline.

How much suffering – car-accidents, divorce, cirrhosis of the liver – could be averted if people lived up to the Qur'ānic injunction against alcohol! (I, at any rate, would not have lost my teeth in my 1951 car crash).

There was a time when my expertise as gourmet allowed me, solely with my taste buds, to identify without fail typical vintages of the *grand crû* red wines of Burgundy's Côte d'Or – Chambertin, Musigny, Clos Vougeot, Romannée, Echézaux, Corton – growing between Beaune and Dijon. Even when first becoming a Muslim, I could hardly imagine going to sleep without a bottle of red wine at dinnertime. Now, however, I sleep better than ever because, while I lie dormant, my circulatory system and liver can rest as well.

Western people cannot believe that a party without alcohol can be fun or enjoyable. They should just watch a typical Islamic wedding!

Most politicians are aware of the grave consequences of Western structural alcoholism: poor public health, reduced labour productivity, security risks at work and on the road, and a waste of economic resources. Yet they fail to muster the necessary determination to fight this "opium of the people". As if it had been expedient, without risk, or popular when the Prophet in Madinah completely outlawed intoxicating drinks and drugs! Nevertheless, the Madinese Muslims poured their stock of palm wine into the gutter, demonstrating that – given charismatic leadership – the unpopular can become popular.

Islamic Brotherhood

Jeddah, 18 December 1982

At passport control, the young Saudi official studies, in turn, our pilgrims' visa and our faces, repeating this procedure enough times that I start to worry that something is not in bureaucratic order. Then I notice tears running down his face. Unexpectedly, he jumps up, leans over the counter, and embraces me as a "brother in Islam".

How often have I met such tears of joy on radiant faces when eastern Muslims recognize me as a believer! If such reactions were still common among Christians, they would understand better why Christian missionary work failed among Muslims. Indeed, a Muslim may be destitute, illiterate and know only two *sūrahs* of the Qur'ān (*al-Fātiḥah* and *al-Ikhlāṣ*), but he will nevertheless feel vastly superior in essential knowledge to any non-Muslim – particularly people whom he sees proselytizing with polytheistic notions such as "son of God", "mother of God", "Trinity", "salvation through divine self-sacrifice", and "sacraments".

The poor, illiterate Muslim quotes: "There is no god but God," and enjoys his conviction that the time of ignorance (*jāhiliyyah*), while not behind everybody, lies behind him.

Pilgrimage to Makkah

Makkah, 20 December 1982

Clad in the simple white garb of the pilgrim, we enter the Great Mosque (Masjid al-Ḥarām) and find ourselves facing the Kaʻbah at the centre of a vast inner courtyard. This is the moment even a Muslim hardly dares dream about before it happens. When seeing for the first time architectural or natural monuments with which one is familiarized through photographs and films, one is often gravely disappointed. Vision does not meet reality. In this case, however, it is different.

There is no commercial buzzing around this mosque, nor is there a hot, sacred, or magical atmosphere. Everything is light, dignified, and intensely aesthetic.

The large gathering of pilgrims is neither loud nor oppressive. On the contrary, they perform their communal prayers in unison: in a complete silence that protects every person's individuality. Ten thousand pilgrims and visitors silently circumambulate the Kaʻbah. The effect is hypnotic.

We enjoy the precious feeling of being welcome, fully secure among brethren. What "*salām!*" (Peace be with you!) means, here seems to be materialized. Dignity, aesthetics, faith, internationalism. We are particles of a large cosmopolitan unit. In Makkah, racial differences disappear. Only during prayer, when bowing, can I gather from differently coloured feet that all races and continents are present.

The Ka'bah, prototype of any three-dimensional object, in its utter simplicity, is Islam's answer to the quest for a visual symbol of God's perfection. If He – as Ibn Sīnā points out – is simplicity in the highest degree, then this empty, undecorated, rough cube symbolizes Him better than any other realizable architectural device. The Ka'bah represents a "still point" and, in as much as it serves as *qiblah* (global focal point for the direction of prayer), a symbolic anchor of a world religion that knows only too well that God is neither West nor East but beyond the restrictions of time and space.

Next to this architectural solution for a "house of God", Gothic cathedrals and Baroque churches pale into the insignificance of knick-knacks.

After the ritual walk seven times around the Ka'bah (*ṭawāf*), under a starry sky, we stop at the Black Stone (*al-ḥajar al-aswad*), which was placed here by Muḥammad, and has become the object of much kissing and wailing. This custom is at the root of much prejudice by people who would never consider that Christian pilgrims in Rome are engaged in the worship of a piece of metal when kissing Saint Peter's big toe.

No one should nourish such a suspicion when seeing the pilgrims in Makkah, even though goddesses cast in stone had indeed been popular in pre-Islamic Arabia. While symbols may emancipate themselves from their underlying ideas, they will not necessarily do so. Every single "*Allāhu akbar!*" ("God alone is great!" in Lawrence of Arabia's translation) is a living denial of the alleged adoration of a simple black stone.

Straight back to Abraham

Makkah, 20 December 1982

Then, with the help of a Saudi guide (*muṭawwif*), we perform the ageless ritual of *sa'y* – those seven speedy one-way trips between the stylized mounts of Ṣafā and Marwah, both situated within the Great Mosque. How painful it must be for him to hear us mispronounce the ritual Arabic texts with our horrible accents!

Soon we have accomplished all the duties of the Lesser Pilgrimage ('*umrah*). Symbolizing our return to normality, a little boy helps us cut off a lock of hair, and I can finally exchange the rather impractical garments of a male pilgrim for my usual wear.

The next day, hoping for once to be alone in this overpowering Mosque, we get up extra early (around 3 am), well before the first call to prayer. But it is useless, for day and night, streaming without interruption, hundreds of Muslims perform *ṭawāf* or wait in line to touch or kiss the Black Stone once again. In doing so, these Muslims establish a personal relationship, a line of communication, not only with the millions of Muslims who came here before them (and will come here in the future, *inshā' Allāh*), but also and especially with the Prophet. Indeed, when the Ka'bah had to be reconstructed after a flood, it was Muḥammad who, acting as a mediator, pushed the Black Stone into its current position in the eastern corner of the building. Such historical consciousness is typical of a religion whose rites of pilgrimage hark back to Abraham (Ibrāhīm), with a perspective of some 3800 years – provided, of course, that the individual pilgrim is sufficiently knowledgeable about the historical and symbolic connotations of the rites he performs.

The Christian churches do not readily admit how many Jewish and heathen traditions they incorporate. Islam, however, makes no bones about the origins of its rites. Muḥammad, peace be upon him, never pretended to be the founder of a new religion. His mission was simply to reconstruct and complete the one and only religion: submission to God, namely, ageless Islam.

Next to the Prophet's grave

Madinah, 23 December 1982

If one has witnessed the ardent nightly *mevlut*-celebrations that take place in Turkey on Muḥammad's birthday, one will be particularly impressed by the resolution with which Saudi religious police in Madinah assure that no one will say his ritual prayers facing the Prophet's grave, and that only individual informal prayers for his soul are spoken near his tomb.

One cannot quarrel with this attitude if one is aware of Jesus' posthumous career – a process which, at first propelled by adoration, finally culminated in the outright deification of this prophet.

In Islam, as well, such tendencies must be kept in check to prevent them from gaining momentum.

Mishap in the hotel

Madinah, 24 December 1982

This year, on a Friday and Christmas Eve, the authentic birthday of Muḥammad and the fictitious birthday of Jesus coincide. As we enter the dining room of the Madinah-Sheraton for lunch, a smiling Pakistani waiter wishes us a friendly "Happy Christmas!" Since this hotel is situated outside the Ḥaram-district and is therefore accessible to non-Muslims, he has understandably taken us for Christians.

When I reply, equally warmly, "By the way, and *al-ḥamdulillāh*, we are Muslims," the poor waiter and his colleagues are mortified. Soon the hotel manager comes and begs us, as a small compensation for so terrible an insult, to have this meal, and teatime, "on the house". As if Muslims were not obligated to honour Jesus as a prophet, nor instructed to believe in the genuine revelations of the Bible!

It just goes to show that Muslims, on average, know as little about the New Testament as Catholics do about the Old Testament.

On covering women

In the evening we walk towards the Prophet's Mosque – over-decorated and a bit too flamboyant for my taste – in order to offer the *maghrib* prayer. My wife and I must separate. She disappears among a crowd of hundreds of identical-looking women, all veiled and covered by the same black *'abāyā*-tunic.

Afterwards, acutely aware of a change of roles, I patiently wait for her to pick me up at a street lantern. (The alternative procedure – me trying to identify my wife – would have been too risky in a country in which men do not address women.)

While waiting, I ponder on the pros and cons of the Wahhābī custom of veiling women so totally – a custom that is not Arab but Byzantine and Iranian in origin. Women of leisure and high social standing had obviously found out that they could underline their "class" by taking to the veil. Making them seem slightly remote, this device would make them appear more rare and precious. And of course, cultivating the veil simultaneously enhanced the Oriental proclivity for jealously. At any rate, it is a fact that at the time of the Prophet and immediately afterwards, Muslim women were not totally veiled (and Bedouin women in Saudi Arabia are still not). Indeed, women pilgrims to Makkah must not be veiled because their predecessors, contemporaries of the Prophet, were not when they went on pilgrimage.

On the one hand, it is not without logic that Saudi women go voluntarily beyond the Qur'ānic obligation to cover themselves. If the purpose of covering a woman's hair, bosom and arms is to save her from becoming a sex object, to protect marriages from unabashed solicitation, and to avoid a vain and ruinous beauty and fashion competition among women, then why should such strong points of sexual fixation as eyes, mouth, and ankles remain on public display?

On the other hand, the history of fashion provides us with ample evidence that veiling can be extraordinarily enticing, and that the fix-points of male sexual preoccupation themselves undergo periodic changes – as is well demonstrated by the historical process of shortening the female skirt during the 19th century. Today's scandal is tomorrow's boredom.

One may argue that the question of where to draw the line is of little or no relevance. There is some limit to stripping, isn't there? If this is accepted, the actual line drawn – full or partial veiling – is of secondary importance.

The Islamic solution to this problem must be derived from two major principles: to observe measure and moderation, and to balance purpose and means. Consequently, most Muslim women cover themselves sensibly and adequately in accordance with sound prescriptions in the *Sunnah*.

By shunning total veiling, they stress that the stability of their marriages is not just a function of unavailability of other "chances". It would be a shame, would it not, if Muslim partners remained faithful to each other only for lack of sexual comparisons! That a Muslim woman chooses to cover herself is not a symptom of immaturity on her or her husband's side. Quite the contrary.

Lost in prayer

Madinah, 26 December 1982

Goodbye visit to the Prophet's Mosque

Today it took much longer than usual to evacuate the building after prayer. Something seemed to be blocking the main entrance. Right in the middle of the stairs, a Muslim was totally absorbed in prayer! Probably, he had arrived late, shortly before the final "*as-salāmu 'alaykum*" (spoken by all first to the right, then to the left), and he was now catching up on what he had missed. Concentrating on his prayer, he forgot everything around him.

Everyone – keeping well out of his way – took good care not to disturb him. Similarly, nobody made critical remarks about the delay that he was causing. He was doing his duty, no more. Such a scene could, of course, never happen when Christian pilgrims overcrowd St. Peter's in Rome. This difference may be due to the fact that in Christian liturgy only the sacramental mass performed by a priest has the status of formal ritual. In Islam, there is one and the same formal ritual for all. The *imām* only "leads" the others in prayer in order to assure uniform timing.

Prayer in Islam enjoys the highest stature and rank. All comprehensive textbooks of Islamic law, such as the authoritative 13th century compendium *Minhāj al-Ṭālibīn* by al-Nawawī, devote their opening chapter(s) to it. In the earliest of such works, namely Imām Mālik's *Al-Muwaṭṭa'*, no less than the first fourteen books deal exclusively with the conditions and rules of prayer. According to these rules, every Muslim must strictly respect the peace and quiet of a person who is praying. The necessary space for prayer – whether or not it is marked off (for instance by the size of a real or imagined prayer rug or simply by a pair of glasses deposited in front) – must not be violated under any circumstances. Assured of such civility, which can be observed in any Islamic country, it is relatively easy for a Muslim to focus deeply on his prayer – whether at a petrol station, on a pavement, or even high up on a scaffolding.

The strength of Islam is often seen in the West as a riddle. Yet this strength is arrived at openly. It results from the ability to pray.

Worries about the validity of prayer

Badr, 27 December 1982

On our return trip from Madinah to Jeddah, we approach Badr, the very place where, in 624, the entire fate of Islam seemed to depend on the outcome of a mere skirmish. Our bus driver frequently gauges the position of the sun. When it had clearly passed the zenith – no more danger of sun worshipping – he stopped the bus and invited all passengers to pray the noon (*zuhr*) prayer.

As we formed a long single row along the road, my neighbour, a South-African Indian, admonished me gently not to forget to take off my sunglasses. Otherwise, during prostration, I could not, as required, touch the ground with both forehead and nose.

I found this remarkable for several reasons. Firstly, a Muslim entirely unknown to me had worried in a most brotherly way about the validity of *my* prayer. Without becoming improperly righteous, he had followed the basic Islamic command to promote what is right and to prevent what is wrong. Secondly, he had demonstrated that detailed knowledge of every rule of prayer is common among Muslims of every nationality and walk of life. And thirdly, he had underlined that praying in Islam is an occupation actively involving both the spirit and the body – so much so, by the way, that a new Muslim will suffer many muscle aches.[2]

A mature Muslims's prayer – like his view of all things and his personality – is integrationist. Submission implies prostration, and vice versa.

---

2. Doctors are aware of this. Indeed, during my physical checkup in 1983, my "habit" of praying was positively noted as "daily gymnastic exercises".

Islam and the oil boom

Jeddah, 28 December 1982

Twice in history the Arabs drew the lucky lot: in the 7th century, when Islam made the globe revolve around Makkah; and again after 1973, when oil prices rocketed. When God mandated the Arab Prophet to "Recite in the name of the Sustainer...!" (96:1), He made a gift of permanent value. The discovery of oil, however, was more of a mixed blessing.

If one lives in the Hijaz, both events may well engender dreams of belonging to a "chosen people" of Arabic denomination. Yet my young Saudi friend, Rafiq Banawi and his colleagues, are unaffected by the new riches. Their dignity – the heritage of free Bedouin families – is independent of bank accounts. They are not fascinated by the dollar rate, spot market prices or the sexual liberation, as propagated by Herbert Marcuse. They prefer to discuss religious issues, and, every morning, they telephone each other to make sure that none of them oversleeps the early *fajr* prayer.

In the West, one often wonders for how long such rigorous puritanism can withstand the onslaught of luxuries. One cannot imagine that in a situation of opulence decadence can be staved off.

Of course the Saudis do not re-enact all the stages of industrialization; they abruptly enter the technological age at its post-industrial stage. The question is whether this phenomenon increases or decreases the danger to religion posed by a high standard of living.

Before speculating further, one must realize just how Marxist this approach is! Have we really become so imbued with materialism that we can no longer conceive of a rousing idea that could be more than a mere superstructure (Marx's "*Überbau*"), a mere reflection of prevailing economic conditions?

In fact, Islam is more than a function of class stratification and per-capita income. It is a religion that can provide considerable immunity against the idolatry of wealth and comfort. Indeed, a good Muslim will not adjust his priorities to market criteria. He resists the compulsion to optimize production and maximize profit. At the same time, Muslims neither demonize nor disdain private property, commerce, profit, and wealth. Like a business manager of the Catholic order Opus Dei, a good Muslim feels at home in the economic world without prostituting himself in obedience to the utility principle.

On these grounds, there is justified hope that Islam, avoiding the excesses of the Western and Marxist-Leninist civilizations, will emerge the better alternative, the one with a human face.

Submitting one's intellect

Aachen (Aix-la-Chapelle), 5 February 1983

During the annual Spring meeting of German-speaking Muslims in Aachen's Bilal Mosque, someone challenges the compatibility of my position as NATO Information Director with my Islamic convictions. I, however, see no difficulty in reconciling these two roles. Indeed, if Islam is to grow in the West at all, the West must, above all, be secure from Soviet expansionism and intimidation. This greatest of external dangers – even for the Islamic world – is contained and neutralized by the Atlantic Alliance.

I admit, of course, that the Soviet Union, as the leading power of world Communism, poses a lesser ideological problem for Islam than Western agnosticism, materialism and technology. Western "scientific" atheism comes silently on little cat feet (to borrow Robert Frost's words), whereas Soviet "scientific" atheism is brutally imposed by Red Army tank divisions, as in Afghanistan. Nevertheless, any spiritual rejuvenation in the West, including the readiness to opt for Islam, presupposes physical security against Soviet intervention. Therefore, the political interests of NATO and the Islamic nations currently coincide.

I am also expected to explain my personal "road to Mecca". Well, here is what I said:

"When I read the Qur'ān for the first time, I was immediately impressed, even struck, by a statement in verse 164 of the 6th *sūrah:* 'Nobody shall be made to bear another's burden.' I mistook this as a moral (and most un-Christian) rule rather than seeing it correctly as a theological reality: that man and woman face their Creator directly, without any possibility of intercession. 'Who is there that could intercede with Him, unless by His leave?' is the precision given in the Verse of the Throne (2:255). 'Not to bear another's burden' has a second, equally fundamental implication: the denial of the concept of Hereditary Sin. If one does not proceed from the assumption that we are desperately in need of 'salvation', one will not search for a 'saviour' and is unlikely to find one. Hence, this single Qur'ānic statement throws a great deal of light on the mechanism that can lead to the derailment of Christianity.

"Having understood this, I also realized that Islam was not retrograde, but rather that it had moved mankind forward, beyond the stage it had reached after Jesus. Using Hegelian and Marxist terminology, Islam put Christendom back on its feet after having stood on its head.

"Agnostics, while claiming that we cannot know anything with certainty beyond the reach of our sensual perception, generally proceed to assert that there is 'probably' no reality beyond. This is not an intelligent but an unjustified, biased position. It would be far more honest to maintain that, on the basis of human intellectual inquiry, we cannot establish probabilities regarding the unseen.

"Having assumed this latter position for a while, I suddenly realized intuitively that the limits of what we can know are not the limits of reality. This was a decision to believe. I had been so impressed with our severely limited ability to perceive anything reliably that I preferred a position of humble dignity to a position of stupid pride – the position assumed by supposedly daring and self-sufficient agnostics who all too often live in icy, narrow self-isolation.

"Thus, I consciously submitted myself, including my intellect, to the larger reality of which I felt myself to be a tiny part. I submitted to what is greatest among what is greater than man: God. *Allāhu akbar kabīran* – God is greater than the greatest (we can imagine).

"In saying this, I do not want to lead anyone to the slippery slope of defining God anthropomorphically. It is one thing to enumerate the 'Ninety-nine most beautiful names' (attributes) of God, and it is another to be under the illusion that these allegorical attributes, coined in human language, sum up and describe His nature and being. In as much as we are slaves of our self-made vocabulary, even with the help of revelation we can only catch a glimpse of God's incomprehensible reality."

To have said more would have been less.

Breakthrough for Islam

Bonn, 4 June 1983

The best that could happen to Islam in Germany at this juncture has happened: a Protestant professor of theology, Dr. Paul Schwarzenau, has written a "Qur'ānic Guide for Christians" (*Koran-Kunde für Christen*, Stuttgart 1982) in which he upholds the truth of the Qur'ān, even where it is in conflict with the Bible.

Schwarzenau, indebted to C.G. Jung's analytical psychology, recognizes that the Qur'ān reflects archetypes that are consonant with the "collective unconscious". This leads him to assert that the Qur'ān is pure, unfabricated revelation, historical and at the same time independent of any historical context: timeless, condensed truth. He compares the Book with a rotating, multi-faceted crystal that mirrors God's light in countless reflections.

In short, Schwarzenau arrives at the conviction that Islam is the primeval religion, primeval monotheism, and therefore both the oldest and the youngest religion. (If nothing else, this would seem to make a true Muslim of this Christian professor!)

Schwarzenau, of course, does not accept the Trinity as implying Jesus' consubstantiality with God, stating: "The historical Jesus would never have tolerated a deification of his person." He adds that, in this respect, the New Testament has been falsified through false interpretation if not through forgery.

Could anything better have happened for Islam this year?

Clean, cleaner, cleanest

Bonn, 16 August 1983

Whenever one despises a member of another race or creed, one finds that one can "smell" him. In short: the enemy stinks.

The Germans felt this way about Poles and Jews, even while it is proven, even statistically, that German cleanliness pertains more to scrubbed pavements and windows than to scrubbed teeth. Currently, Germans discriminate against Turkish guest workers. They are different and therefore suspect. In short: they must be dirty.

The Turks are not immune either from this psychological trap. They now also turn up their noses when they see those "dirty" rich Arab tourists taking up all the benches near all the best hotels along the Bosphorus.

This kind of racial self-delusion is grotesque, particularly when Muslims are targeted, because Islam places the greatest possible stress on cleanliness. To say that a Muslim must pray is as much as to say that he must wash. Islamic law even requires that husbands and wives take a bath and wash their hair every time they have intercourse.

I can honestly say that I have not infrequently been bothered by bad-smelling people at the Paris Opéra, at the Lincoln Centre in New York, and at the Munich National Theatre, but never in a mosque.

Could it be that Muslims are the cleaner Germans?

Homegrown Muslims

Bonn, 14 September 1983

The Diplomatic School of the Foreign Office in Bonn
has, for the second time, organized a seminar on aspects
of Islam. In 1980, Muhammad Rassoul made an appearance.
This year, the F.O. is mustering three homegrown Muslims:
M.A. Hobohm, Rolf Abdullah Behrendt, and me. My lecture
is based on the manuscript of my forthcoming book entitled,
On the Role of Islamic Philosophy, due in 1985 (English version:
Cologne 1985, ISBN 3-8217-0043-2).

At lunchtime we cause some embarrassment when we
refuse pork. Do people here still ignore the fact that the
consumption of pork is not only pernicious if the meat is
trichinous, but that it also accumulates cholesterol, slows
down the body metabolism (with the ensuing risk of
intestinal cancer), and often causes furuncles, eczema, and
rheumatism? Is it not relevant that dangerous influenza
viruses live through the summer thanks to the hospitality
of pigs? Apparently not, for in 1983, with the breeding of
80 million pigs, the production of pork reached an all-time
record in the European Community.

If one lives without pork for a while, one develops a
strong antipathy to the smell of this meat, even nausea. And
if one accidentally consumes pork – if only some fat – one
is likely to get stomach ache.

Strange that the uneducated, illiterate, "backward" Muḥammad should have anticipated all this? Must have had an intelligent informant...

Linguistic trickery

Bonn, 19 November 1983

Islamic fundamentalists are often accused of primitive hair-splitting and of taking Qur'ānic texts too literally. It is, however, sheer defamation to claim that fundamentalists simply overlook the fact that a great part of the Qur'ān cannot be understood literally. They know only too well that metaphysical reality can only be transmitted to us, if at all, in linguistically coined images derived from our (gravely limited) sensual perception.

To admit that the cosmological and theological passages of the Qur'ān are necessarily allegorical in nature is one thing; to foster the illusion that anyone could be capable of fully understanding those revealed allegories is another. Fundamentalists categorically deny this possibility.

Thanks to pioneers of linguistic analysis such as Fritz Mauthner and Ludwig Wittgenstein, it should by now be common knowledge that all our thinking, dreaming and feeling (including knowing "intuitively" or through "illumination"), takes place, if at all, within the framework and associations provided by our languages. Consequently, there is not either any doubt about the fact that every single word, even so-called "abstract" terminology, is a product of sensual perception channelled into vocabulary. We cannot say what we cannot think, or think what we cannot say, and both activities revolve exclusively around our sensually perceived "reality".

Against this background, fundamentalists are convinced that metaphysical facts can only be transmitted, as part of revelation, in allegorical or metaphorical form, and that there is no reliable way, neither through logic nor sufism, to penetrate the imagery of revealed texts.

To put it bluntly, if it is a sign of intelligence to respect the narrow limits of human sensual perception — as modern scientists do — it cannot be a sign of stupidity if one applies this same cautious skepticism towards any metaphysical inter-pretation of the Qur'ān — as fundamentalists do. Faced with the problem of unravelling dark, ambivalent or symbolic passages of the Qur'ān, fundamentalists, in philosophical terms, are absolute critics of metaphysics, religious agnostics, or skeptical nominalists. They soberly acknowledge that both philosophical discourse and mystical visions of metaphysical matters, because of the incapacity of our self-produced vocabulary, are likely to be mere babblings.

Seen from this angle, are not fundamentalists the really far-sighted, clear-eyed and judicious ones?

Something uncanny about it

Bonn, 29 December 1983

Many have tried to retrace the life of Muḥammad, his "path" (*sīra*) between 570 and 632 AD. Two biographies are, however, exemplary: Ibn Isḥāq's classic *Sīrat Rasūl Allāh*, in the form given by Ibn Hishām around 200 AH (translated by A. Guillaume, Oxford 1955), and Martin Lings' recent *Muḥammad, his life based on the earliest sources* (New York 1983).

Leaving aside what a propensity to see miracles and a tendency toward political partisanship may have contributed, Muḥammad emerges from those sources as a statesman-like personality of great charisma, will power, and tactical prowess.

The period between his emigration to Madinah and his peaceful conquest of Makkah one decade later, shows him to be a strategist to be mentioned in the same breath as Carl von Clausewitz. Muḥammad had already consciously applied economic and psychological warfare and used arms control negotiations as an instrument of foreign policy. The armistice he accepted at Hudaybiyyah – to the consternation of his entourage – was a diplomatic *coup* of the first order, and the Makkans soon realized that they had signed themselves into future capitulation. Equally extraordinary was the Constitution of Madinah, dictated by Muḥammad as a federative treaty between the Muslim and Jewish communities.

If one also takes into account Muḥammad's success in trade and commerce, his wisdom as judge and arbitrator, and the stylistic power and beauty of his pronouncements, one is at a loss to explain how an uneducated, illiterate, "backward" Arab could possess such qualities.

There is something uncanny about it.

There is something Divine about it.

Muslim pluralism

Lützelbach, 16 February 1984

A year ago, Ahmad von Denffer published twelve *Briefe an meine Brüder* ("Letters addressed to my Brothers"), subtitled "Towards a Muslim Community". He combines a radical appeal to live up to the demands of Islam – to really give priority to one's faith – with concrete suggestions for how to arrive, step by step, at individual perfection within a closely-knit Muslim community (which might as well be called Muslim Brotherhood).

Such initiatives have a strong tradition. All through Islamic history, young Muslim men created "virtuous" societies, often secretive ones, based on the guild system (*al-futuwwa*).

Considering human inertia and egoism, it has never been easy to achieve religious momentum. However, Ignatius of Loyola and Vladimir Ilyich Lenin managed to make the world budge through the creation of "cadres". Similarly, improving the chances of Islam in the West takes more than the total commitment of a few; it also requires organizational and logistic skills.

Today, we meet in a small circle in the *Haus des Islam* (House of Islam), located in this small Hessian village south of Frankfurt, to discuss how to achieve official recognition of Islam in Germany. Such recognition is a prerequisite for the introduction of Islamic religious instruction into schools and for the collection of "church taxes" through the financial administration of the State.

The pre-prerequisite of such a breakthrough is, however, that Islam in Germany speaks with one voice. Understandably, the German authorities want to deal with a single solid partner. And there is the rub!

Indeed, Muslims, like the Arabs, are a fiercely independent lot. They practise a pluralism that no church would either allow or survive. This diversity may be affected by the absence in Islam of sacraments, and hence of priests and bishops. (Access to sacraments and clerical office has often been used to enforce uniformity and discipline.) At any rate, even under the leadership of a caliph (i.e. until shortly after World War I), Islam always showed extreme tolerance in matters of legal and theological interpretation. A factor contributing to this situation must, of course, be seen in the injunction against "excommunicating" someone as long as he clings to the very basics of Islam and alleges that he is a Muslim. It is, indeed, a rarity that, as in Pakistan, a sect deriving from Islam, such as the Aḥmadiyyah, is officially outlawed.

Muslims have always considered their motley variety as a strength rather than a weakness – whether their four legal schools (*madhhab*), their religious orders (for example, the Qādiriyyah, the Bektashī, the Naqshbandiyyah), or their sects (such as the different branches of Shī'a).

In the West, Muslims are additionally divided into groups on the basis of ethnic or language affinities. The result is an often confusing spectrum of Islamic organizations, cultures, and creeds living under the great dome of Islam.

If all these splinter groups would heed Ahmad von Denffer's advice, Muslims in all European and North-American countries would soon realize that they are sitting in one and the same boat, and are rowing in the same direction, together.

The American prophet

During the Spring Conference of NATO's Foreign Ministers, we stay in a Washington Marriot Hotel belonging to a Mormon family. The Book of Mormon of the Church of Jesus Christ of the latter-day Saints is therefore deposited in the drawer of every bedside table. Its text, in Biblical language, was supposedly found by Joseph Smith in, of all places, Palmyra, New York, in 1830 and, of all things, on golden tablets (which, conveniently, disappeared immediately).

Today, several million people believe in this "American revelation", thus giving additional evidence that nothing can be so absurd that it would not be held as true by someone. (*Credo quia absurdum?*)

A religion as sober as Islam can, of course, not compete with such wondrous tales, nor does it wish to.

I put the book back into the drawer, spread out my prayer rug from Konya, and pray my night prayer – just before I am floored by the jet lag resulting from a ten hour intercontinental flight.

Circumcision

Istanbul, 9 July 1984

To be circumcised as a grown-up person is no child's play, even if it is carried out by a surgeon in a modern hospital in Nişantaş.

Circumcision is a highly symbolic act. One takes part in a tradition and joins a chain that goes all the way back to the Prophet Ibrāhīm, more than 3000 years ago. Submission to Allah (islām) is to be as irreversible as the physical results of circumcision.

Circumcision is not mentioned in the Qur'ān. It is a tradition, instituted by the Old Testament, and dealt with in ḥadīth-literature in the context of other good habits of personal hygiene like cutting hair and fingernails. It is therefore quite certain that the popularity of the custom of circumcision has further, much deeper roots. The justifications given by modern parents for the circumcision of their boys – arguments of a practical, hygienic and sexual nature – only scratch the surface.

Superstition

Istanbul, 15 July 1984

Islam is inimical to any form of superstition, but it would be an illusion to believe that Islamic countries were free of the evil eye, magic powers, and sorcerers "blowing on knots" (mentioned in *Sūrah al-Falaq*, 113:4). The Qur'ānic injunction against a soothsayer's fortune telling has not even reduced the semi-serious custom of reading one's future from the bottom of a coffee cup.

Many enlightened Turks seem to have shed Islam but not their vulnerability against, and sensitivity to, superstitious practices, thus confirming the saying "where there is no faith, there is superstition".

Curiously, some measure of activity, even bordering on magic, infiltrated the texture of Islam itself in connection with the ambivalent role played by *Sūrah Yā Sīn*. Its citation, particularly by a *hoca*, in favour of the living or the dead, is considered particularly effective.

But what is one to make of it if this, or any other Qur'ānic text, is worn as an amulet? Is such a defence against fate not a weapon forged against God's providence? Some women in Turkey can even be caught brewing *sütlü Yā Sīn* (*Yā Sīn* milk), supposedly exerting healing power or guaranteeing immunity against *nazar* (the evil eye).

Man is, of course, inexorably prone to manipulate his own (or others') fate, knowing the future, or mobilizing forces in his support. It is sad that Islam has not been able to eradicate this weakness. Should it have been repeated even more often in the Qur'ān that "nobody knows the hour", that Allah rewards and punishes as He wills, and that nobody can intercede without His leave?

Is this religion – Islam – too sober? Do some of the faithful miss a Byzantine God on a golden mosaic background? A crucified God whom they could touch? A baby God in the manger?

A'ūdhu bi-llāh (I take refuge with God)!

In victory, ask for forgiveness

Rome, 15 October 1984

Returning from lecturing at the NATO Defence College on "Public Opinion and Defence", I find time at Fiumicino Airport to learn the 110th *sūrah* of the Qur'ān, *al-Naṣr*. I already know the Arabic text and its meaning but am afraid to memorize the wrong pronunciation. I therefore address a fez-wearing Tunisian in the departure hall with an *"as-salāmu 'alaykum!"* The moment he understood my request, he started quoting *al-Naṣr* for me as if he had expected this invitation all along: *"Idhā jā'a naṣrullāhi wa'l-fatḥ ..."* (when God's help comes, and victory...).

According to the last verse of this *sūrah*, in the hour of victory, Muslims are admonished not to triumph but to humbly seek forgiveness. What an astonishing rule! How different might diplomatic history have been if statesmen had more frequently heeded this advice! Could World War II have been averted if Clemenceau and Poincaré, instead of indulging in feelings of hatred and revenge towards Germany, had abided by *al-Naṣr* in 1919?

The Dionysius Areopagita saga

London, 24 October 1984

My uncle, Hugo Ball, founder of Dadaism in Zurich during World War I, is not only remembered for his inventive poetry of sheer sound (*Lautdichtung*) but also for his clairvoyant criticism of past and contemporary society (*Zur Kritik der deutschen Intelligenz*, Berne 1919; *Die Folgen der Reformation*, Munich 1924; *Die Flucht aus der Zeit*, Munich 1927). He should, however, also be given credit for his important contribution to theology presented in his *Byzantinisches Christentum* ("Byzantine Christendom", Munich 1923, 2nd ed. 1979).

This work focuses on Dionysius the Areopagite, a strange saint and author of a theology of angels who, during the Middle Ages, was considered to be a contemporary of St. Paul and, consequently, a witness to the origins of Christianity. Of this and therefore of the authority of his writings, Thomas Aquinas was fully convinced.

While we know less today about the personality of Dionysius (calling him therefore Pseudo-Dionysius), we know much more than Thomas Aquinas ever did about the origins of Dionysius' writings. Whoever he was, he did not live before the late 5th or early 6th centuries, and was strongly influenced by Proclus (*Proklos*), to the point of becoming a pristine Neoplatonist and Gnostic in approach. Thus, what the Church readily accepted among its earliest doctrine, namely Dionysius' "mystical theology", which included his speculations about the hierarchical structure of the cosmos, had in fact been established some 600 years after Christ.

For students of Islam, Dionysius – a Greek sufi – is of great interest if they want to grasp certain aspects of Islamic mysticism and Shī'a doctrine, in particular concepts such as "light", "illumination", "super-godhead", "ecstasy" and "unification with God". In honour of Dionysius it should, however, be restated that in his first letter to Gaius he acknowledged that "true perception of God is non-perception". And: "If someone who claims to have seen God understands what he has seen, he did not see Him Himself. Because He Himself is beyond perception and beyond being, He is unrecognizable, non-being, super-being... Total non-perception... is true perception..."

Hugo Ball proved that Dionysius used many notions and concepts derived from Gnostic occultism and Persian light mysteries. These were typical of ancient secret cults cultivating fantastic cosmological theories, particularly about the nature, status, number, function, and hierarchy of angels. These ideas have left their mark in the Christian world, in as much as they proceeded from the assumption that matter in general, and the sensual part of man in particular, were inferior or even evil. This Manichaeism, this demonization of the world, served as the foundation for a superstructure of higher spheres through which man could ascend towards salvation and sanctification.

All these notions are only a short step away from the interpretations given by the 11th century enigmatic doctor of Islam, Abū Ḥāmid al-Ghazālī on the basis of the Qur'ānic Light Verse (24:35).

Many know this versatile philosopher, jurist and theologian for his "destruction" of metaphysical speculation, *Tahāfut al-*

Falāsifa, his orthodox *Iḥyā' 'Ulūm al-Dīn* (The Revival of Religious Sciences), and his sober, rational "Confessions". But as evidenced by his *Mishkāt al-Anwār* (The Niche of Light), al-Ghazālī was also a Sufi.

Today, at long last, I found this book in an Islamic bookshop in London's Seven Sisters Road, in an English translation by W. Gairdner. Waiting for my return flight at Heathrow Airport, I virtually devour it.

Drawing heavily on Gnostic and Neoplatonic speculations that are typical of pseudo-Dionysius' thought, al-Ghazālī dares to interpret several rather dark and ambiguous words appearing in the Qur'ān. He takes, for instance, *al-rūḥ*. Is it to be understood as soul, spirit, divine inspiration or personified as Holy Ghost? Or *al-muṭā'* (he who is obeyed): Gabriel, Plato's demiurge (builder of the universe as God's vicegerent, not its creator) or the First Emanation? *Logos*, which could be taken literally, as word, but also as personified Word of God, soul of the universe, being, emanation. Or *al-amr*: is it God's command, the command of the demiurge as prime-mover acting on God's behalf? Even *al-nūr* can be seen as light, as God himself, Muḥammad, or as the Neoplatonic demiurge.

In these attempts to define Qur'ānic terminology, the idea of demiurge appears repeatedly. This is no mere coincidence. It was after all central to Gnostic and Neoplatonic thinking to conceive of a God, Highest and Immovable, who is above the act of creation, creating therefore only indirectly via a second level "prime mover".

It takes little imagination to realize that al-Ghazālī's mystical visions – verifying this type of cosmology – moved him too close for comfort into the vicinity of accepting what would amount to a "Son of God", thus nearly violating Islam's most basic doctrine of *tawḥīd*.

For a moment at least, al-Ghazālī seems to have pushed aside the fundamental rule for interpreting Qur'ānic terms: "He it is who has bestowed upon thee from on high this divine writ, containing messages that are clear in and by themselves and these are the essence of the divine writ – as well as others that are allegorical. Now those whose hearts are given to swerving from the truth go after that part of the divine writ which has been explained in allegory, seeking what is bound to create confusion, and seeking its final meaning; but none save God knows its final meaning…" (3:7).

Tell me about the relationship between a Muslim Sufi, Greek-Persian Neoplatonism and Gnosticism, and I will tell you what I think of his views.

They thought I was joking

Brussels, 27 November 1984

As chairman of the annual NATO conference of Heads of Information from Ministries of Defence, I provided participants today with an analysis of medium-term trends in public opinion.

I tried to put my finger on symptoms of a gradual change of consciousness, particularly among members of the next generation. I see many of them as idealists yet pessimistic moralists who foster post-materialistic values, show a particular need for togetherness, and a readiness to follow emotionally strong leadership. Their willingness to submit is glaringly obvious during any rock concert. Moreover, many of these young people seem disillusioned and disaffected. They have no confidence in democracy, State institutions, or in public or private authority in general. For these and other reasons, they harbour grave misgivings about the future.

During my presentation, I point out the fact that these phenomena are but the tip of an iceberg of deeper socio-cultural disruptions – realities that were long predicted by alert observers such as the Harvard sociologist, Daniel Bell (*The Cultural Contradictions of Capitalism*), and the Belgian professor, Léo Moulin (*L'Aventure européenne*).

I associate myself with their analyses of the current stage of explosive scientific and technological expansion.

According to them, Western society, characterized by pluralistic democracy, the rule of law, and technological orientation (in other words, a fully industrialized capitalist market society), owes its development to the respect for, and application of, Judeo-Christian values as shaped by humanitarian and liberal influences. These values were all initially founded on religious convictions and norms, such as the uniqueness of the human soul, the brotherhood in Christ, God's command to till the earth, and virtues such as diligence, parsimony and delayed gratification. But it has become obvious that the Western economic upswing tends to torpedo (or poison) itself the more successful it is. The higher the standard of living and general prosperity, the more this system undermines the foundations that had so far undergirded it.

In this process, old values tend to become perverted. Individualism can turn into narcissism; self-determination into anarchy; tolerance into value neutralism; flexibility into disregard for any tradition; prosperity into hedonism; diligence into consumerism; parsimony into workaholism; competitiveness into cut-throat competition; sensitivity into squeamishness; brotherhood into totalitarianism; equality into uniformity; and confidence in God into a no-risk mentality.

In short, I described symptoms of creeping structural decadence in the Western world and asked whether our democratic mechanisms were flexible enough to cope with such change? Or whether the West could fall victim to its own flexibility?

The valiant information officers around the table did not know how to react and therefore maintained a long, embarrassed silence. They had not been prepared to listen to an analysis of public relations problems that would pinpoint the decline of religion in the West as a major issue.

Then one delegate took heart and asked whether there was a chance for religious revival in the West? I answered that I saw no chance that the existing Christian churches could become relevant again for the majority of the young. I also denied the feasibility of creating a new Western ideology through sheer sociological engineering, and added: "As the so-called underground churches of the young and youth sects prove, this generation feels a strong need for ideological and religious bearings. Currently this potential is vagrant – shifting between Marxism, ecological freaks and Hare Krishna. However, it is not excluded that this urgent quest for religious commitment and fulfilment will lead to the adoption of an altogether different non-European religion that appeals to the young as an antidote to materialistic woes, stressing brotherhood, excluding religious hierarchies, and being naturally affirmative of life: Islam."

My listeners took this as a joke. I did not.

Women in Islam

Lützelbach, 24 December 1984

Young German Muslims who recently embraced Islam are gathered in this "House of Islam" in anticipation of their departure for Makkah on *'umrah* (lesser pilgrimage). The atmosphere, however, is tense, because the Saudi Arabian Embassy is not authorized to issue visas for some women in the group who are unmarried and unaccompanied by a close male relative (as their fathers and brothers are not, yet, Muslims).

The Saudi Arabian Foreign Ministry routinely refuses access to single women, fearing an influx of single girls in pursuit of a prince and an oil well. The traditional rules of Muslim law governing both *'umrah* and *ḥajj* pilgrimages also do not allow participation of unmarried women unless they are accompanied by close relatives. A sensible rule in view of all the logistical and climatic hardships of pilgrimage, but an absurd rule in the present circumstances. (Muslim jurists in earlier centuries simply could not imagine a case in which a female pilgrim would be the sole Muslim in her entire family!)

Thanks to the patient *démarches* of Muhammad Siddiq, a German *imām* trained in Madinah, the Foreign Ministry finally finds a way out of the dilemma, and, after a short delay at least some elderly German women pilgrims are able to join their group in Makkah.

Non-Muslims usually assume that women are not allowed into mosques or on pilgrimage. Some people even still believe that women in Islam are thought to have no souls. How disturbed can man's relationship to reality become! How grotesque that such legends continue to live on in the face of clear evidence to the contrary!

In Islam, women are not only seen as possessing a soul; they also enjoy the same religious status as men, and therefore must, if possible, perform the pilgrimage. According to David Long, *The Hajj Today* (Albany, N.Y., 1979), in 1972, 170,864 of the 479,339 pilgrims to Makkah, namely 34.6%, were female. And while it is true that when praying in a mosque, women do not mingle with men, this is very much like Catholic women who used to occupy only the left side pews when attending mass.

In other respects too, Muslim women have enjoyed during the last 1400 years a legal status that their European sisters only obtained with difficulties during the 20th century. Marriage, for instance, has no negative consequences whatsoever for a wife's property. She, and only she, can continue to administer, and dispose of, her pre-marital property as she sees fit. And separation of property (instead of male tutelage) – a recent European achievement – has always been the legal regime under Islamic Law.

Similarly, even if it is true that sons inherit proportionally more than daughters, husbands alone provide for the upkeep of the entire family. And if the wife is unwilling to breastfeed her baby, her husband must pay for a wet-nurse. She has the last word in questions of child raising, and if necessary, she can sue for divorce herself.

As a matter of principle, women are not barred from any usual profession. During the Battle of Uḥud (in 627), Muslim women fought as combat support troops, and the Battle of the

Camel (656) was even *pro forma* commanded by a woman: 'Ā'ishah, the Prophet's wife.

There are other, debatable points concerning the equality of sexes in Islam. Nevertheless, the critic should absorb the facts that are mentioned here before he or she launches a wholesale attack on Islam in pursuit of women's emancipation.

Where mystics err

Aschaffenburg, 26 December 1984

L ike all Sufis, Idris Shah knows that one cannot be initiated into the mystical path by reading books. Yet, he profitably issues one publication after the other on the wisdom of dervishes and magi. His writings nevertheless throw some light on the tried and proven methods of Sufism, more perhaps than historical-scientific analysis of the phenomenon of mysticism can render, particularly *Mystical Dimensions of Islam* (Chapel Hill, 1975) by the leading Western expert, Prof. Annemarie Schimmel (Bonn and Harvard universities).

It can only be applauded if people in search of God utterly distrust human logic and intellectual rationality as instruments of metaphysical perception. However, entering another dead-end street cannot be the alternative to entering a blind alley. That the rational approach to the problem of ontology does not lead very far, does not imply that the irrational approach will lead any further.

On the contrary, inner vision cannot succeed where sensual perception fails because, in the last analysis, inner vision is itself nothing else than a by-product of sensual perception. Any mystical experience is valid only in as much as it can be formulated in one of our languages. Therefore, even illuminations resulting from ecstasy are predetermined by, and take place within, the narrow framework of linguistic concepts derived from sensual experiences. In other words: the inner path is no alternative at all.

There is no escaping the limitations of our sensual apparatus. There is no rationality or irrationality devoid of sensuality. There is no illumination free of predetermined associations – all provided via the vocabulary of our self-produced languages.

At any rate, there is no way of verifying the ontological truth of what a mystic believes he sees with an inner eye and hears with an inner ear. Sufis claim that they can easily detect impostors. People in general are, however, so eager for panaceas and miracles that they would invent their own *marabouts* (as popular saints are called in North Africa) – on whose graves one can attach snippets of one's clothes – if charismatic personalities of wisdom did not in fact appear.

Extreme skepticism is in order whenever Sufis show a desire of mystical union with God because this may nourish a pantheistic illusion of identity, whereas the God of Islam, Allah, is a transcendental god. The pantheistic form of *shirk* caused by mortal man's desire to enter into God's presence prematurely, is alarming enough. Worse, however, is the Sufi allegation that some of them, given the right method and dedication, can obtain better knowledge of God through special, private illumination than through what has been revealed for all through God's prophets. This is arrogance bordering on blasphemy.

Men and women, as created by God, the Perfect One, are not misfits, misconstructions, or machines with inborn defects. Humans are characterized and distinguished from animals by their rationality. Is it conceivable, then, that they could serve God well only if they abandoned this rationality in favour of irrationality?

Similarly, I do not believe that the body of revelation, foremost the Qur'ān, transmitted for the use of mankind, is a coded occult message full of secrets and therefore truly accessible to only a few members of an esoteric elite. Is it Islamic to turn Islam, this middle-of-the road religion, into the privilege of a pious aristocracy?

Biblical evidence

Geilenkirchen, 4 February 1985

In his book on "Biblical Evidence" (*Das Zeugnis der Bibel*, Weilerswist 1984), Sahib Mustaqim Bleher identified those passages of the Old and New Testaments that contribute to a verification of the Qur'ān in general and of Muḥammad's prophetic mission in particular.

Contemporary Western Muslims expect too little of a comparative study of the Bible and the Qur'ān as if, as Prof. Hans Küng keeps pointing out, Islam and Christianity could not throw a great deal of light on each other's origins. (Credit must be given to Christian theologians such as Adolf von Harnack, Adolf Schlatter and Paul Schwarzenau, for having admitted that the Qur'ān preserves the earliest and most correct interpretation of the status, role and nature of Jesus and therefore reminds and confronts Christians with their own past.)

Western Muslims seem, nevertheless, preoccupied with one connection between the New Testament and the Qur'ān: the prediction of Muḥammad's mission in John 14:16 and 16:13. Muslims agree (and Prof. Küng concurs) that a correct reading of these verses – Periklytos (i.e. Aḥmad in Arabic) instead of Parakletos – amounts to more than a mere hint that (1) there will be another prophet after Jesus, and (2) that he is Muḥammad. It is perhaps equally important to agree on how John 14:26 must *not* be translated, namely Parakletos (helper) as "Holy Ghost" in the sense given by the doctrine of the Trinity. Indeed, in clear contradiction to John 16:13, many editions of the Gospel accept this latter translation and thus represent a further infiltration of Hellenistic and Gnostic preconceptions into this (anyhow suspect) text. (As if the Evangelist's Gospel had not been falsified enough by Christological manipulations.)

One may, of course, legitimately ask whether it is not sufficient to see the Qur'ān as a self-contained, self-verifying whole. Do prophets require a particular pedigree?

Is it helpful to underpin the Qur'ānic revelations with documents which, like much of the Bible, and particularly the Gospel according to St. John, are themselves badly in need of verification?

Rationality, freedom, and love

Brussels, 7 February 1985

Marcel H. Boisot hit the issue squarely on the head with his essay on "The Western Value System: A Moral Weapon" (Journal No. 3/84 of the European Institute for Security in Luxemburg). Analyzing the current situation of the Western value system, he concludes that civilizations always head for disaster if, as the West does today, they allow three key factors to get out of balance: (1) rationality, (2) freedom, and (3) love.

Freedom untempered by love results in chaotic exploitation. Rationality untempered by love may lead to Holocaust. Love untempered by rationality may become self-destructive. Rationality without freedom is a prescription for the Gulag Archipelago.

Read fraternity (instead of love), respect for accessible knowledge (instead of rationality), and individual dignity (instead of freedom) and you will understand why a truly Islamic civilization can avoid the current imbalance of key factors in the West.

Today, at NATO Headquarters, I distributed this pamphlet to the Conference of National Information Officials, urging them to detach themselves for once from their immediate problems in order to focus on their longer term task: to cope with an almost imperceptible, silent, cultural revolution that is nibbling away at the very foundations of the Western value system.

If His Honour had only resisted

Brussels, 8 February 1985

When Christians make the mistake of rationally defending the dogma of the Trinity, they first engage in linguistic acrobatics only to finally beat a retreat claiming that, being a mystery, Trinity escapes explanation.

Today's letter-to-the-editor in *Frankfurter Allgemeine Zeitung (FAZ)*, written by Dr. Gerhard L. Müller, is a case in point. This former Chief Justice of Germany's highest labour court explains that the Church had at no stage conceived Jesus as being of mixed nature, half God and half man. "The connection between God and man (in Jesus) is of such a unique kind that one cannot find an analogy in the history of religions." (Mr. Müller errs. Religious atavisms are never spun so fine.) Müller goes on to say that Jesus was recognized as God "because as pre-existent Son of God he always existed in God and remained God while accepting humanity from Mary," namely "through God's own Spirit." "This event amounted to a fresh start for mankind, irreversibly set in motion by Jesus."

Wow! If His Honour had only resisted joining together so much artificial vocabulary void of meaning! (Or should Muslims be thankful for so much inadvertent advertising?) Would it not have been preferable (and more dignified) to plead intellectual bankruptcy when asked to explain the Trinity?

It would, of course, have been even better if Mr. Chief Justice had delved a bit into the fascinating history of the notion of Trinity – be it composed of Isis, Osiris and Horus, or of God the Father, Mary and Jesus, or of God the Father, Logos and Jesus. For, in that case, he would have had to admit – like St. John, St. Paul and pseudo-Dionysius before him – that he had succumbed to playing a language game first played by Plato and the Gnostics.

It is a banality to state that mysteries are inexplicable. They are by definition. However, we are never barred from establishing whether what is presented as a mystery is one or whether, like the Trinity, it is a speculative construction of human hearts and minds.

There was a time when Christendom could profit from the dogma of the Trinity, especially when proselytizing among peoples who believed in a hierarchy of gods. Today, the Trinity is a burden for Christianity.

Islamic democracies?

Brussels, 14 February 1985

Saudi Arabians are regularly defamed as "puritan fundamentalists". This is an odd concept if it refers to their efforts to combat superstition and corruption. Indeed, it is with this in mind that the Saudi authorities fence off the so-called "grave of Eve", mother of mankind, in Jeddah and discourage hero-worship (or worse) at the historical cemetery of al-Bāqī' in Madinah.

Such an accusation is also odd if it refers to the Wahhābī reform of mores in Makkah. For, as we know in detail from Heinrich von Maltzan (*Meine Wallfahrt nach Mekka*) who smuggled himself into the Holy City in 1860, it sported at that time opium dens, brothels, and robbers' nests.

Finally, it seems rather rash to me that the Saudi way of life should be defamed because of the unusual habit of taking religion as seriously as Christians used to do once upon a time.

If puritan fundamentalism connotes an absence of complacency and hypocrisy, then yes, there are such fundamentalists among the Saudis, and they can be proud of it.

They may feel that moving forward ("progress") in a specific situation like ours today requires the adoption of a model tried and proven in the past. After all, such an attitude – constructive conservatism – is a position respected in the West, provided it is not held by Muslims.

It is certainly not primitive to defend the hypothesis that the solution of societal problems found by Muḥammad and the first four caliphs might serve as a model for the solution of the problems of post-industrial societies. Nor is it naïve to endorse, as the Saudis do, a negative attitude towards speculative philosophy and theology as defined by the philosophical school of al-Ash'arī (874–935 AD). Is this fundamental critique of philosophical ontology and metaphysics primitive simply because it was formulated centuries before David Hume, Immanuel Kant and Ludwig Wittgenstein?

In the last resort, Western critics of Islamic fundamentalism focus on the attitude of Islam towards the Western model of pluralistic parliamentary democracy. They overlook the fact that many Western liberals and socialists comfortably live in constitutional monarchies that give Christianity a privileged legal status without being feudal. Islam, too, does not impose autocratic theocracies.

It is not conclusive to point out that the history of Islam is not a history of democratic development. Christians frequently suffered under evil "illuminated rulers", "enlightened kings", "God-fearing emperors", and "vicars of God"; and Islamic peoples all too often had to put up with evil and arbitrary sultans, caliphs, and emirs. Indeed, the legal history of Islam can be seen as one long struggle between a liberating idea – the rule of Islamic law, assuring equity, equality, and security against arbitrariness – and brutal factual despotic power. Reason enough for Prof. Karl J. Newman to ask in today's *Frankfurter Allgemeine Zeitung* "whether there is one single non-dictatorial State today under the Crescent?"

Yes, Islam still owes mankind an adequate and concrete proof that a modern Islamic state (or a "theo-democracy" as Mawdūdī calls it), in theory and also in practise, can assure a participatory rule of law in accordance with both the Qur'ān and the bill of basic human rights.

No hit, no danger

Brussels, 25 February 1985

No professionals have suffered as much under terrorist attack as diplomats have during the last two decades. Consequently, they receive much expert advice on how to escape being blown up in their car, being kidnapped or shot by snipers.

Yet, even if I fully followed their counsel, it would not add one second to the span of life accorded me. A bullet that missed, even a close shave, was never really a danger, and a bullet that hit could not have missed.

This does not imply that a Muslim should not acquaint himself with the advanced features of a Heckler & Koch P7 M14 pistol. But he should never be under the illusion that his days are not counted. "*Innā lillāhi wa innā ilayhi rāji'ūn*" – "Verily, unto God do we belong and unto Him shall we return" (2:156). And: "No human being can die save by God's leave, at a time preordained" (3:145).

I did not have this permission to "return" when American and British bombs rained down on my home town every fortnight during World War II. Nor did I have it when surviving my car crash in Mississippi on 26 June 1951. Nor did I have it fourteen days later when, during my return trip to Washington, a lunatic in Tennessee put a bullet through the window of my train compartment, inches away from my head. I did not even have it when I was to be posted as ambassador to Jeddah in 1976, and they discovered that I had a cancerous tumour on my left kidney. *Kismet*.

A standing invitation

<hr>

Brussels, 9 March 1985

<hr>

The 17th International Book Fair in Brussels' Centre Rogier
concentrates on publications in French and Dutch. An
optimist, I look for new Islamic literature. The computer at the
information desk, under the entry *"islamique"*, sends me to a
stand specializing in esoteric and occult writings, including
books on whirling dervishes and the equivocal pranks of
Nasreddin Hoca. Only at the display of German books can I
find a few items produced by the Cologne publishing house,
Islamische Bibliothek.

In view of the strong competition of other missionary forces
here, this is a shame. Indeed, not only Communist countries
but also pseudo-Christian sects "of the Holy Grail", Islamic
heretics such as the Daheshists, astrological circles, and
homosexual pressure groups occupy a whole floor of the Centre
Rogier.

Stout Belgian women, members of the Baha'i movement,
exude a humanistic enthusiasm reminiscent of Schiller and van
Beethoven's "Be embraced, millions!" Do Muslims lack the
imagination, enterprise, and organizational skill displayed here
by the adepts of the late Baha'ullah? Or is it below the dignity
of Islam to be seen joining ranks, as even the Catholic Church
does here, with dubious fringe groups of an underground
counter-culture?

Indeed, Islam does not favour aggressive, systematic missionary work. It is a religion that places its trust on the inevitable attraction of the exemplary lives of individual Muslims. Catholic style *propaganda fidei* is atypical of Islam. Rather, it perceives itself as a standing invitation, an open door-religion with permanently outstretched hands and a self-explanatory message. In other words, it counts on the automatic effect of its simplicity, naturalness, clarity and sobriety on those who are willing and able to hear and see.

Such an attitude makes sense if one believes that God, and He alone, will lead to the straight path (*ṣirāt al-mustaqīm*) whom and how He wills. Against this background, peddling Islam on street corners may in fact seem out of place.

But faith is one thing and fatalism another. A Muslim should indeed be conscious of the fact that God is the original cause of all events. However, he should not resist becoming a link in a chain of causality leading to the conversion of his neighbour. He should always pray as if it was his last prayer, and yet plan and work as if he were to live another fifty years.

In this respect, Muslims can learn from Marx's deterministic philosophy of historical materialism ("histomat"), which might also have served as an excuse for a passivist stance. Yet Lenin imbued Communism with Bolshevic activism. Party cadres served to help along "inevitable historical processes", voluntarily speeding up the course of history as it heads towards its predetermined goal of full Socialism on a global scale.

Yes, Muslims, too, should allow themselves to be instrumental in the spreading of their faith (*da'wah*), according to their best judgment and their best abilities.

Oh, she said

During a diplomatic dinner, my Spanish neighbour at the table learns that I am Muslim. "Oh, she says, you are one of those who still wait for God to be born." For a moment, realizing how thoroughly Reconquista had managed to distort the image of Islam, I remain speechless. Then I consider quoting from the 112th *sūrah*: "He begets not, neither is He begotten." Instead, I change the subject, remarking only that "this is the one thing Muslims are not waiting for!"

Had I not learned in etiquette class that matters of politics, religion, and health should be avoided at the dinner table?

Four nightingales from Istanbul

A concert cycle in the Protestant Church near Place Royale is to present sacred music of the great world religions. The programme could well have used Hugo Ball's motto: "Art is much closer to religion than science." Today, we are to witness a guest performance of the "Muezzins from Turkey" who present Qur'ān recitations in Arabic and, in Turkish, poems by Süleyman Celebi (14th century CE) which are parts of the Ḥanafī celebrations of the Prophet's birthday (*mevlut*).

The organizer first explains the difference between instrumental Sufi music and the unisonal chanting of these four *muezzins* that builds on the internal rhythm and word melody of the Qur'ānic texts. He concludes by asking us to refrain from applause because such sacred music should not be distanced from its real content and purpose: prayer.

These four "nightingales", thanks to their big and clear but also nasal and pleading voices, are expressive indeed. Many in the audience are deeply touched by their utter concentration and earnestness. Elements of the best in Islamic art!

Nevertheless, I remain uneasy. Should one serve the Qur'ān aesthetically decorated so that it can be enjoyed *l'art pour l'art*? Did Friedrich Nietzsche not have the right instinct, in the largest sense, when writing in *Die Geburt der Tragödie* (The Birth of Tragedy) that true Christendom "negates all aesthetic values"?

Hearing the words "Allah" and "Muḥammad" appear equally often, did people here not find their misconception confirmed that Muslims, in analogy to Christians, were "Muhammadans"?

And are the Wahhābī Muslims not right when discouraging even an aesthetically pleasing rendering of the two calls for prayer, *adhān* and *iqāma*?

Did we today not reach the point where art dominates and submerges prayer, where art becomes an obstacle to prayer?

Brotherly love vs. brotherliness

Good Friday, 5 April 1985

It can be taken for granted that newspapers such as *Frankfurter Allgemeine Zeitung* and *Die Welt* will devote a page to Christian teachings at Easter. It cannot be taken for granted, however, that such daily newspapers focus on Islam as "the fastest growing religion everywhere", as they did this year.

Too bad that the chance was missed to underline common ground between the Jewish, Christian, and Muslim faiths. Karl-Alfred Odin wrote: "What separates them is the idea of how God is God. According to the Christian formula, God is Love..." (*FAZ*, 4 April).

Odin is right when using the term "formula" because that is exactly what it is, and no more. But he is not right in terms of argumentation: "Dying on the cross, symbol of the suffering of humanity, God saves mankind by burdening Himself with this suffering." To be brutally simple: The Christians' "loving God" is either identical with Allah, the Compassionate and Merciful, or he is not God at all.

An analysis of the concept of "love" brings it all to light. Human beings associate love with a desire to give themselves to, and to fuse themselves with, another person. Consummate love needs a response, love in return. A lover and his partner accept each other as being at the same level, but they also put each other on a higher pedestal and need one another, becoming dependent of each other in the best sense.

God obviously cannot be loving in this way. Otherwise, He would not be the Exalted, Perfect, Absolute, Sovereign, and Independent Being that He is. It is indeed blasphemous to argue that God without a "Thou", without His creatures, would be poorer. God was before all time and creation, and was always Perfect.

God's love for His creatures can therefore only be conceived as an unequal relationship, which does not detract from the almighty sovereignty of Him Who eternally rests in Himself. This means that God can be benevolent, compassionate and merciful towards His creation if He so wills, but can also be just and punishing if He so wills.

When Christians refer to their God of Love they usually do not think of God the Father but of Jesus who could, as a man, be a sacrifice and even sacrifice himself for his brethren. God, however, while He may accept sacrifices, does not need them. A necessity for Him to sacrifice Himself (or part of Himself) to Himself would be in contradiction to the divine nature of the One Whom we call Jehovah, God or Allah. God is free to forgive if He so wishes, without any conditions or procedures. Christians are proud of the "epochal breakthrough" represented in the concept of a God of Love. In reality, as far as the philosophical and theological concept of God is concerned, this was an enormously retrograde step. All the progress already made thanks to the Greek thinkers and Jewish prophets was jeopardized by the Christian notion of an incarnate God with human features. Then as now, Christians projected their fear-inspired wishes onto their concept of deity, rationalizing away the awe that inevitably results from an unobstructed view of the Divine. If Jesus achieved a historical breakthrough, it was due to his command to love God and one's neighbour as one loves oneself. But it would be sheer defamation to deny that Islam incorporates these very commands. Christian "brotherly love" and Muslim Brotherliness are one and the same thing.

Not stupid and yet Muslim?

Brussels, 9 April 1985

Every week I host one or more lunches at NATO Headquarters for groups of visitors invited by the NATO Information Service (NATIS). The waiters are accustomed to place a bottle of mineral water in front of my place instead of wine. They also discreetly swap pork dishes for something else. Many guests observe this manoeuvre.

When I explain that my "diet" is due to the fact that I am, *al-ḥamdulillāh*, a Muslim, most people first think that I am joking, particularly if they had shortly before heard me giving a competent briefing on subjects like "East-West Relations", "Problems of Arms Control", "Alternative Strategies", or "Public Opinion". (Not stupid and yet Muslim?)

Curiosity signals the next stage. People ask: "What (the hell) moved you to become a Muslim?"

This is followed by a third stage of inquisitive conversation characterized by an airing of prejudices and subliminal fears about Islam. Here are the most typical clichés: holy war, polygamy, and Khomeini!

With considerable patience, I try to explain that "holy war" is Western terminology. The Islamic concept in question, *jihād*, at its root means no more than moral endeavour. I also point out (after a sniping remark about the Crusades) that, according to verse 2:256, Islam does not permit coercion in matters of faith.

I readily admit that the theology of Sunnī and Shī'ī Muslims may diverge more drastically than that of Catholics and Protestants.

When addressing the Islamic law of matrimony, I draw my guests' attention to the possibility of the first wife's excluding any others in her marriage contract. I also assure my listeners that in today's highly sensitive society it could only exceptionally be feasible to conform to the Qur'ānic conditions for having more than one wife, verse 4:129 predicting: "It will not be in your power to treat your wives with equal fairness, however much you may desire it."

Normally, these table conversations end in a tie. What more can I expect than to gain a tiny bit of respect for Islam?

Young visitors, however, are quite attracted by a specific element of this religion: that a Muslim meets his God as an emancipated human being without the intervention of hierarchies. No wonder. These youngsters have a particular axe to grind with rituals, traditional formalities, and bureaucratic structures.

Small as my chances are, I never give up hope that some of my guests, during our luncheon conversations, may catch a glimpse of the crystalline spirituality of Islam, and may recognize that this religion represents a zenith of human intellectual and moral achievement.

Allah knows best.

The Bible, the Qur'an and Science

Brussels, 11 April 1985

Maurice Bucaille's *Bible, Qur'an, and Science*, subtitled "The Holy Scriptures in the Light of Modern Scholarship", is a remarkable affirmation of the sources of Islam. Most orthodox Jews fail to recognize to what extent the Old Testament is human literature, man-made, so that it is quite impossible to filter out what can safely be regarded as revealed.

The same can be said of Christians. They seem to suffer a mental block whenever they are confronted with the truth that the New Testament, including the four Gospels, in many respects is not an eye-witness account but second-hand hearsay commentary. The interpretation of the role of Jesus that is typical of today's Christianity had in fact been suggested by Hellenistic partisans of St. Paul's extremist school, which was dominated by Neoplatonic and Gnostic ideas. This faction was so successful that they pushed their Judeo-Christian opponents not only off stage, but out of memory.

Bucaille first enumerates the many cases in which the Bible is in contradiction to proven facts, such as the sequence of creation, the genealogy of Jesus, and the dating of specific historical events. He also mentions the better known inconsistencies between the various Evangelical accounts of the Resurrection and the Sacrament of the Eucharist.

Bucaille confesses that he had himself been dumbfounded when he first discovered that the authenticity of the Qur'ān could not be attacked on the basis of identical or similar weaknesses. He was further surprised to learn that, on the contrary, there is not a single Qur'ānic statement that would not stand firmly under scientific scrutiny – whether a statement relating to cosmic, genetic or deep-sea research. The Qur'ān even pronounces itself correctly on details of embryonic development – facts that could only recently be verified thanks to intra-utero microscopy.

This is the backdrop for Bucaille's assertion that, "in my opinion, there is no natural explanation for the Qur'ān." That the author, on the other hand, found much medical nonsense ascribed to the Prophet by weak *ḥadīth*-traditions only strengthens this assertion.

Alas, Bucaille – like Muhammad Iqbal before him – is so eager to discover further evidence of scientific truths in the Qur'ān that he falls into a self-made trap. When seeing, for instance, a prediction of modern astronauts and space research in verse 55:33, he finds only what he himself had deposited through a redefinition of terminology. This approach creates the danger that some readers of the Qur'ān might treat it as an oracle, and fail to remember that theological truths, not scientific ones, are by the very nature of revelation its primary subject. Scientific discoveries cannot invalidate genuine revelation; but the Qur'ān is not either a compendium of physics, biology and chemistry.

Islam and stress

Bonn, 14 June 1985

On mission to Bonn, I run into my old colleague, Dr. Alois Mertes, State Minister in the Foreign Office. Being a slave to his engagement calendar, he must rush off after only two minutes' conversation. The following day he collapses. Infarctus. Dead.

Too much stress?

All Western languages now use this term as if it explained, in and by itself, the damage resulting from self-destructive living. Yet, the prototype of modern man, the business manager, does not work much more than people used to in previous times. What is new, and makes stress a recent phenomenon, is modern man's feeling of not being able to cope, of living under a constant pressure to over-achieve. Many people in the West see only one alternative: fight or flight. They no longer realize that there is a third option: to flow.

In their fight for more money and success (and against time, circumstances, and their bosses), managerial types end up fighting the limitations of their own bodies by using various kinds of narcotics: alcohol, cigarettes, tranquillizers, pep-up and sleeping pills. The predictable results are physical wrecks – heart, lungs, liver, circulatory and nervous systems all in a terrible shape. Sensible doctors therefore ask their patients to stop drinking, smoking and stuffing themselves with pills, and to resort to tranquillization through "transcendental meditation" (TM).

For me, this whole phenomenon is one more proof that the Islamic way of life accords with man's God-given nature, and that Islam is perfectly relevant for a solution of today's health problems. In fact, it is no overstatement to point out that a real Muslim cannot be a stressed personality, and vice versa.

Alcohol?	Forbidden
Nicotine?	Highly suspect because of the danger of factual polytheism implied in any form of addiction
Cholesterol?	Without pork, a manageable problem
Overweight?	Reducible through fasting during Ramaḍān
Fear of failure?	*Allāhu akbar!* Only God's judgment counts
TM?	What else is praying five times a day?
Time is money?	Not for a Muslim
Physical fitness?	Muslim prayer has this side effect
Circulatory stimulation?	Islamic ritual washing stimulates the autonomous nervous system.

Does this checklist not provide firm evidence that living in accordance with the Qur'ān and the *Sunnah* is a healthy life, and one more reason to see Islam as a drugless antidote for the structural problems of modern industrial society.

Being myself a manager, I know what I am talking about. But I am a manager with a prayer rug in his bag.

Hazreti Atatürk and
other curiosities

The story is being spread by word of mouth that a miracle has happened. And, indeed, if you drive from Edremit along the Aegean Sea towards Ayvalık, near Gomec you will see, with your own eyes, that the silhouette of the mountain chain to your left has assumed Atatürk's profile!

One can only congratulate the founder of modern Turkey, for this particular landscape resembles his rugged features remarkably. People now predict that the same phenomenon is about to occur in other parts of the country. It seems that Mustafa Kemal is launched on a second career: sanctification. Will we one day have a *Hazreti* (saint) Atatürk?

This allows me to understand even better why Islam is so intolerant of statues depicting the human form. You never know the career they might make.

Near Ayvalık, above a bay almost cut off by the sea and therefore called Ölü Deniz (Dead Sea), tourists flock towards a protruding rock called the Devil's Pulpit (*Şeytan Sofrası*), where the mischief-maker left a practical hoof imprint, just the right size for sacrificing small coins.

It is all very funny. And the less people believe in the existence of Satan, the more popular he becomes. Baudelaire therefore paid Lucifer a compliment: "To convince people of his non-existence is the devil's masterpiece!" (The same could be said, I suppose, of the KGB!)

One should of course know that Shaytān, the fallen angel Iblīs, is seen by Muslims as a tempter only, and not, as in Persian and old Germanic mythology, as a counter-force to God. Nevertheless, any citation of the Qur'ān (and thus also formal prayer) is always preceded by the imploring formula: "*a'ūdhu billāhi min al-shaytān al-rajīm*" (I take refuge with God from the cursed devil).

After having a swim in Ölü Deniz, at a water temperature of no less than 32°C, we wish to visit the Great Mosque of Ayvalık, a former Greek-Orthodox cathedral. But contrary to Islamic custom it is locked. Indeed, even if Muslims are not supposed to pray (but rather work) between the early morning and noon prayers (namely, a period of 6–9 hours), in contrast to Protestant churches, mosques usually remain open during this period of the day.

The same situation – being locked out – happened to us for the first time a week ago in Üsküdar when we tried to visit the famous, but hidden, Cinili Cami with its 400-year-old blue tiles. In both cases the excuse was the same: danger of carpet theft. Granted. But is it not incommensurate to thus shut the faithful out? Should the mosque not be stripped of all its luxuries and left open instead?

Nostalgia in Üsküdar

Üsküdar, 10 August 1985

If one climbs the slopes of the Bosphorus high enough near Üsküdar, one makes a fascinating find: a restored dervish cloister (*tekke*) that belonged to Muslims from Uzbekistan who were members of the Naqshbandiyyah – a Central Asian dervish order well described by Prof. Dr. Annemarie Schimmel (*Mystical Dimensions of Islam*). Today, this *tekke* is the property of a religious foundation (*waqf*) under the administration of descendants of the Naqshbandī *shaykhs* who now carry "Özbek" as their family name.

Restoration progresses building by building. There are living quarters for men that are separate from (but well connected with) the women's quarters; a small mosque (*mescid*); a spacious kitchen; a romantic courtyard, with fountain and water basin; and an overgrown dervish cemetery – the ensemble would not be complete without it.

If any surroundings exude peace, these do. Just being here amounts to contemplation. It is a place far removed from the busy world. It stands alone, out of time.

It dawns on me that this soothing atmosphere may be what Muslims wish each other when saying "*Salām!*" (God's peace be with you!).

On how to deal with death

Karaca Ahmed Mezarığı, the largest cemetery in the Orient, if not of the entire world, covers much of the wooded plain above Üsküdar. In a large park dominated by cypress trees, for miles, there is nothing but graves, all directed in such a way that the dead – lying on their right side – face Makkah. This parallel arrangement of course cuts right across natural slopes and results in a peculiarly structured and patterned landscape: as if a huge magnet situated in Makkah were pulling and focusing everything in the same direction.

There is a second major visual difference between this Islamic burial ground and a Christian churchyard: the characteristic absence of bombastic monuments and statues (although the Turks are more tolerant of marble than their Arab cousins).

Ostentatious mourning, uncontrolled wailing, tearing one's hair and clothes, any cult surrounding tombstones, any class-conscious perpetuation of human glory beyond death, are all un-Islamic modes of behaviour. Western observers are tempted to misinterpret this restraint as impassivity. Patience in the face of misfortune is confused with heartlessness. As if it had been for lack of respect and devotion that the Saudis, in 1953, buried their beloved king, Ibn Sa'ūd, in an unmarked commoner's grave. No, the correct interpretation of these phenomena is simple: in their negative attitude toward any kind of hero-worshipping of the deceased, Muslims are guided by their obsession not to slide into a violation of *tawḥīd*. They want to underline that even when geniuses, prophets or saints pass away, they do not share God's glory. He reigns without associates.

On the other hand, Westerners frequently overestimate the discrepancies between the cosmologies and eschatologies of Christendom and Islam. Both religions are aware that "as this world is constantly passing away, the other one is constantly approaching" ('Abd al-Qādir al-Ṣūfī). As any good Christian, a good Muslim daily prepares himself for death. This very attitude of alertness has even been institutionalized within the obligatory rites of pilgrimage (*ḥajj*), with the long symbolic wait at 'Arafāt.

The Qur'ān abounds with allegorical descriptions of heaven and hell, and Muḥammad added to this eschatological material the accounts of his vision of a voyage to Jerusalem (*isrā'*) and ascent to Heaven (*mi'rāj*).

As if this were insufficient (and as if more could be known), pious Sufis speculated in fantastic detail on the meaning and circumstances of such symbolic concepts as the trumpet (to be blown before the Final Judgment), and the narrow bridge (which is to be crossed on one's way to Paradise). Publications such as *Totenbuch des Islam* (Islam's Book of the Dead) by 'Abd al-Raḥīm ibn Aḥmad al-Qāḍī (1981) even dare to give a stunningly concrete portrayal of what might be called the geography of the beyond.

However, no amount of these flights of fancy will lead sober Muslims to believe that these authors really know what they are talking about. Such "books of the dead" with all their well-intentioned travel instructions for the passage between life, death and resurrection, only illustrate our incapacity to understand more of life after death than has been revealed unambiguously.

I like to have my feet on solid ground.

My "book of the dead" is the 36th *sūrah* of the Qur'ān, *Sūrah Yā Sīn*.

Meeting Muhammad Asad

Lisbon, 21 September 1985

In Lisbon's Tivoli Hotel, we eagerly await Muhammad Asad and his American wife, Pola Hamida. At long last! He himself drives up, being his own chauffeur at the age of 85. We first speak German – language of his youth – then English. But he would be equally ready to enter into conversation in Arabic, Farsi, French, Portuguese, Spanish or Urdu.

I ask as many questions as I possibly can without being rude in order to find out more about the background of the astonishing scientific and literary achievements he has made for Islam over much of this century. I also remind him of his hope, expressed in the 1930's, that Islam would fill the vacuum left when Western and Communist atheism would both leave the stage in a state of spiritual bankruptcy.

His prediction was partially correct, for both systems are in decline. However, contrary to his expectations, Islam was not recognized as the alternative, because not one Muslim country has developed in such a way that it could be seen, in the West, as an attractive and convincing counter model. On the contrary.

But even at his advanced age, Asad neither indulges in wishful thinking nor nourishes bitterness. His eyes are as alert and skeptical, and his analyses as sound and sober as ever. If there is something incongruous about this soft-spoken gentleman with a goatee, it is the discrepancy between his enormous contribution towards a revival of Islam on the one hand, and his utter, self-effacing modesty and kind-heartedness on the other.

Asad is under no illusion that much more will have to happen before mankind is globally ready for a strategic advance of Islam; and he expects me to shoulder some of the burden.

Allah is with those who show patience in adversity (2:153), and nothing is impossible with Him.

Fingers off the Qur'ān!

Lisbon, 22 September 1985

The new, monumental mosque of Lisbon – a Bauhaus-inspired re-interpretation of Cairo's Ibn Ṭulūn Mosque – was built right opposite the Gulbenkian Museum (whose fabulous collection of Islamic art is an absolute "must").

Currently 15,000 Muslims, mostly Ismāʿīlīs from Mozambique, live in Portugal. (One has to go back 700 years to find a greater number in this country.)

As I approach a bookstand in the mosque, a young fellow intercepts me with a sign of agitation. He had taken me for an impure non-Muslim tourist who should not touch the Holy Book.

To understand this protective reaction presupposes knowledge of the fact that the Prophet said that bodily cleanliness is "one half of religion". Consequently, according to Islamic tradition, Muslims are not supposed to read the Qur'ān unless they are in a state of ritual purity (which is about the same as actual purity). Christians also used to handle their holy book with reverence, when they respected it in a similar way.

When our brothers from Mozambique find out that it was a case of mistaken identity, they bend over backward to make our stay in Lisbon as easy and pleasant as possible. Brotherhood unlimited.

Long march through
the institutions

TWA 815, 9 October 1985

During my fifteen-hour flight from Brussels to San
Francisco (where the North Atlantic Assembly is to meet),
there is plenty of undisturbed time to read up on the
development of Islam in the United States of America. It is the
history of a remarkable metamorphosis.

In 1932, the Black Muslims were founded in Detroit by
"Prophet" Elijah Muhammad as a militantly racist anti-white
organization with para-military characteristics. His "Nation of
Islam" pursued political, that is separatist, goals. But, in an
unforeseen way, even political activists, after visits and studies
in Makkah, turned into religious Muslims. This happened to
the famous/infamous Malcolm X (murdered in 1965), to a
radical with a criminal record like Rap Brown (now Jamil
Abdullah al-Amin), and to Elijah's own son, Wallace
Muhammad.

After having directed the Black Muslims himself for ten
years, Wallace Muhammad drew the right conclusion and,
astonishing everyone, on the tenth anniversary of his ascent to
power (20 April 1985), he dissolved his own organization on
the ground that it was un-Islamic. In its place, he asked his
black brethren, solely on the basis of the Qur'ān and the *Sunnah*,
to integrate themselves as Americans into the general
community of all Muslims, black or white!

It was to be expected that not all former Black Muslims would follow suit. This turn of events was too revolutionary for many. Therefore, a black extremist, Louis Farrakhan, founded a new "Nation of Islam", this one based on violent anti-Semitism.

The image of mainstream Islam of course suffers under such developments. But the future is with the majority of black American Muslims who, more and more, turn to the real sources of Islam. Today untold copies of the Qur'ān, in English translation, are in circulation, distributed at no cost by the five-year-old Tahrike Tarsile Qur'ān organization.

And where would one locate New Era Publications, the world's most diversified and best-stocked distributor of books on Islam and the Muslim world? In Ann Arbor, Michigan, of course. Where else?

Black Muslims, white *imām*

At the hotel information desk, they only shrug their shoulders when I inquire about a mosque in town. All they produce is a "church register" listing 24 different, mostly obscure denominations. But Islam is missing. We do not give up so easily, though, and find an entry in the telephone directory that says: "Islamic Center, 850 Divisadero Street, prayers daily at 1 pm, on Fridays at 12 am". (A strange way of copying the advertisement patterns of Christian churches and fixed times for services.)

The porter is uneasy about the mosque's location. All he says is: "Don't walk there. If you must go, take a taxi, and only during the day time." Which is a code for saying: Watch out! Black ghetto!

Of course, I do walk those 2–3 miles, always in a Western direction, out of Grove Street and beyond Alamo Square. This leads me into a well-to-do black neighbourhood. People are friendly and out-going; they share with me their appreciation of another crisp sunny day under a crystal California sky.

At the Islamic Center, only four black men are gathered for the noon prayer: an elderly white-haired gentleman who is struggling with the Qur'ān in Arabic; a toothless man-about-the house; an arthritic veteran incapable of kneeling or bowing – who later turns out to be the *muezzin* – and Yusuf Simon, a highly intelligent young Shī'ī student of political science. With a flash of humour he paints his situation of triple discrimination: as a black among whites; as a Muslim among Christians; and as a Shī'ī among Sunnī.

When the *muezzin* calls to prayer, I am surprised to hear him begin with the second call (*iqāma*) and conclude with the first one (*adhān*). Not in doubt about how Bilāl (the first *muezzin* ever and also a black man) would have reacted to such a reversal of order, I point out this mistake as gently as possible.

The consequences are unforeseen but logical: the little congregation decides that I am the most "knowledgeable" Muslim among them and therefore designates me – a white man drifting in from nowhere – as their *imām* for today. And so I found myself, for the first time, standing directly in front of the prayer niche (*miḥrāb*) leading the local *ummah* in prayer. Not of course until I had sternly checked, as it is an *imām*'s duty, that my congregation of four had properly formed a straight row...

During the bus ride back, Yusuf and I heatedly discuss the origins of the personal conflict that had alienated Fāṭimah from 'Ā'ishah and prepared the ground for the later splitting off of the Shī'a sect. People sitting near us are perplexed. Do they not realize that racial barriers do not exist among Muslims? Or can't they believe that women played such active and decisive roles in the earliest days of Islam?

Because it must not be true

Oslo, 28 October 1985

In the presence of His Majesty King Olav V of Norway, I have the honour of giving a lecture on "NATO as a Community of Values" to the Military Society of Oslo. As usual, the organizer introduces me on the basis of a *curriculum vitae* supplied by me. Also as usual, the introduction skips two facts: my religion and my publications on Islamic topics.

The same had happened two weeks ago when I lectured in Denver, Colorado (to the Committee on Foreign Relations), and at the Benedictine St. John's University near Minneapolis. In St. Paul, the master of ceremonies even altered my *c.v.* by announcing that I showed "an interest in Islam".

Why this game of hide-and-seek? Do my hosts really assume that the entry "Islam" in my documentation is a typing mistake? Do they consider my religion an embarrassing aberration? Because what must not be true cannot be true?

Pantheism, Hegel, and Gnosticism, say hello!

Brussels, 25 November 1985

For several weeks now, the *Frankfurter Allgemeine Zeitung* (*FAZ*) has served as a forum for a religious debate fuelled by a critique of Leonardo Boff's "theology of liberation" and Urs von Balthasar's speculations on whether or not Hans Küng, the famous Swiss professor of Catholic theology, is (still) a Christian or has in fact become a Muslim. This is a fascinating spectacle.

I wonder whether we are witnessing a media event – just a dialogue among specialists – or an eruption of broader dimension? Did this debate perhaps uncover a religious vacuum, a popular thirst for more dogmatic security? Considering the alarming rate at which Christians desert their faith and their churches, this would not be surprising.

The former German President, Prof. Dr. Karl Carstens, made no bones about this disturbing phenomenon when speaking in Geneva on 29 August 1985: "As far as future developments are concerned, my greatest worries are not atomic weapons…, not environmental problems…, not the population explosion in the Third World. It is my greatest worry that our civilization might lose its religious dimension. That could indeed spell the end for us: man regarding himself as the measure of all things…"

He spoke against a background of depressing data: pollsters have concluded that "religious faith", with only a 14% affirmation, has dropped to the bottom of the value scale among German youngsters. Only 6% of German Protestants and only a quarter of German Catholics continue to frequent their churches regularly. Many of the young who are seen to be active in West and North European churches are there for political reasons only.

For a Muslim, this intra-Christian debate is of particular interest because both Boff and Küng put the discussion of the nature of Jesus – man and God inseparable in one person? – back on the agenda, almost as if the disastrous councils of Nicaea and Chalcedon had not occurred. In this context it becomes obvious that any justification of the concept of the Trinity, even today, cannot amount to more than stammering.

Look, for instance, at the latest version of the Catholic catechism for adults, and its mystical approach: "Grace is God Himself in his auto-communication through Jesus Christ in the Holy Spirit. Grace, in the deepest sense, means that God accepts us unconditionally, affirms and loves us through Jesus Christ in the Holy Spirit, and that in this love we are *fully one with Him, in personal community and friendship with God, personally participating in God's life.*" For blasphemous pronouncements such as those printed in italics, the Muslim Sufi al-Ḥallāj was executed in 922.

With shells of empty vocabulary chained together by word acrobats, this catechism tries to make the alleged status of Jesus – as consubstantial Son of God – more palatable through bringing all human beings nearer to that status.

Pantheism, say hello!

Noteworthy as well is Prof. Dr. Hans Waldenfels' intervention in the new debate about the Trinity (*FAZ*, 24 November 1985).

For him, the incarnation of God is "a radical fact," God, through becoming man, "fully divesting Himself of Himself." Waldenfels concludes with a monstrous proposition that should have made his pen curl in disgust: "He, God, through incarnation became someone else."

Hegel, say hello!

In another letter-to-the-editor published the following day, the author adopts a position typical for the *illuminati*: "Christ's message does not address reason... It is a message for ... our souls." "God previously created us as perfect children of light, as purely spiritual beings..." The writer does not tell us how, by-passing the mind, messages reach our soul.

Gnosticism, say hello!

But this is not even the peak of recently published absurdities, which was reached, with the French historian, Jean Delumeau's book *Ce que je crois* (Grasset 1985). He correctly proceeds from the assumption that Christian dogma revolutionized the vision of God so radically that, at any time, only a minority of Christians was capable of realizing it. But then Delumeau supports the flawed Christian idea that, since Jesus Christ is God, God is impotent (*non-puissant*), subservient, and suffering. In fact, according to him, God continues to suffer with, and in, all those wretched and miserable people with whom Jesus had identified. This leads Delumeau to express his hope that much will change for the better once people understand "that God suffers with us – and more than we – under all the evil in this tormented world." Morality as pity for God?

In contrast to such fables, the Islamic concept of God is undiluted, coherent and clear. It is a picture drawn by Him of Himself in the Qur'ān: the One, Indivisible, Non-Begotten and Non-Begetting, the Creator, the Perfect, Incomparable, Sovereign, Absolute, Who is neither in need of Perfection nor of His own creation. Allah, the Omnipotent, Who guides man through His prophets without the need of incarnation, procreation, or self-sacrifice.

In view of so much recent Christological speculation, it is as relevant as at any time during the last 1400 years to cite *Sūrah al-Ikhlāṣ,* the 112th *sūrah* of the Qur'ān:

Say: "He is the One God:

God the Eternal, the Uncaused Cause of All Being.

He begets not, and neither is He begotten; and there is nothing that could be compared with Him."

In the eye of the beholder

Brussels, 29 November 1985

Within one and the same week, both *Time* Magazine (2 December 1985) and the *Frankfurter Allgemeine Zeitung* weekend Magazine (No. 300) deal with the phenomenon of Hasidic settlements in Brooklyn (*Time*) and Jerusalem's Mea Schearim quarter (*FAZ*). Both publications describe in some detail how these orthodox Jewish fundamentalists of eastern European origin strictly adhere to their rigid laws governing food and women's dress. They also talk about the separation of men and women during ritual worship and family celebrations, such as weddings. The intensity of the Hasidic's study of the Bible and the Talmud, within the limits of their equivalent concepts of *taqlīd*, is also related. Both periodicals remark as well on the exclusivity and suspicion with which Hasidic communities defend their age-old way of life, in particular their Sabbath customs.

What is striking about all this is the favourable attitude shown by both magazines when they comment on Hasidic behaviour. They concede to them a "positive force" (*FAZ*). *Time* even writes the following based on Lis Harris' book, *Holy Days: The World of a Hasidic Family*: "Though the Lubavitchers are oblivious to feminist concerns, Harris sees humanness in their way of life and says women create an almost 'Amazonian' sisterhood among themselves. Men honour their wives, and there is no observable infidelity."

In other words, what in other circumstances would be branded as discrimination, virtually finds approval as a positive differentiation of the roles of men and women.

"Hear! Hear!" one is tempted to shout. Can one imagine how the very same phenomena would have been received by those periodicals if the fundamentalism under scrutiny had not been Jewish but Muslim? Against a Muslim background, the very same rules and traditions would have been condemned as hopelessly narrow-minded, fanatical, anti-rationalistic, obscure, and a violation of women's right to equal treatment.

Legendary facts

In the train to Hamburg, 4 December 1985

On my way to giving a lecture at the German Armed Forces' Defence College in Hamburg-Blankenese, I read Kamal Salibi's book, *Die Bibel kam aus dem Lande Asir* ("The Bible came from Arabia", London 1985). Based on a linguistic analysis of geographic names, this book, by a Protestant Lebanese professor, presents a stirring thesis on the origins of Israel.

In contrast to traditional Biblical scientists, he takes the historical authenticity of Biblical tales for granted, but not the geography traditionally associated with them. This inventive method leads him to the conclusion that the history of the early Jewish tribes before 500 BC mainly took place between Ta'if and North Yemen, namely in today's Saudi Arabian province of Asir. He also proves that hundreds of settlements, rivers, and mountains in Asir carry names whose sequence of consonants corresponds to equivalent names in the Bible, and that these places in their distance from each other also validate descriptions in the Old Testament. In contrast, Salibi can find very little similar evidence in Palestine.

If it is true that the substance of the Hebrew Bible, including monotheism, took shape in Western Arabia and that Abraham lived there, the "legends" of Islam about the foundation of Makkah by Hājar and the construction of the first Ka'bah by Ibrāhīm and Ismā'īl gain tremendous credibility.

Israeli scientists of course vehemently try to refute Salibi's affirmations since they fear for the legal basis of the state of Israel. As if it were necessary for any people to live in a particular region for more than 2500 years in order to establish a respected homeland!

Salibi's critics point out that quite a few ancient appellations can be found both in Palestine and in the Southern Hijaz region. But this is not conclusive. It is common knowledge that emigrants like to transfer to their new home the names of towns they had used "back home". Just think of Bismarck, North Dakota, or Athens, Pennsylvania.

More important still, Salibi's method enables him to verify much of the Qur'ānic narrative about Jewish prophets. These Qur'ānic accounts of events in Biblical times are not just truncated Biblical material gathered from hearsay (as some Western experts want to believe). Rather, the Qur'ān, according to Salibi, contains independent, original versions of Biblical events.

Moreover, he not only locates in the Asir region the first Jerusalem (al-Sharim, 35 km north of Nimas) and the Garden of Eden (the oasis of Junaina in the Wadi Bisha basin), but also Sodom and Gomorrah and the original Jordan "river" (in reality the mountain slope of Sarat). If his linguistic research holds up, Salibi, with one stroke of genius, has historically undergirded much of the Bible and the Qur'ān, including all the traditions that connected both the Mosaic faith and Islam with Abraham, their common spiritual father, who lived in the area of Rijal Alma and the mountainous region of Qunfudha, south of Ta'if.

In other words: his research provides additional legitimacy for the rites of pilgrimage of Makkah, 'Arafāt, Muzdalifah and Minā.

Human rights and Islam

<hr>

In the train to Brussels, 5 December 1985

<hr>

In the November 1985 issue of '*Arabia*', Fathi Osman makes the point that contemporary Islamic thinking is rather vague about how to see essential human rights from an Islamic perspective (p. 11). Alas, he is right.

When Muslims are questioned about their attitude toward the basic achievements of the 18th century American and French Revolutions, the echo can be disconcertingly ambiguous. On the one hand, there are sovereign Muslim intellectuals, such as Muhammad Asad and Fathi Osman himself who, without being modernist revisionists, openly and unabashedly deal with the question of whether Islam, its essence and rationale, remains relevant for our age. On the other hand, one can find an author such as Oğuzhan Şimşek who, in the 1 November 1985 issue of *Hicret* (Cologne), makes short shrift of democracy by stating: "*Demokrasi nedir? Islam değildir.*" (What is democracy? It is not Islamic).

Further, Islamic States do not react uniformly to the codification of human rights, be it the Universal Declaration of Human Rights by the United Nations General Assembly (10 December 1948), or the International Pacts on civil, political, economic, social and cultural rights (19 December 1966).

Egypt, Iraq, Jordan, Lebanon, Libya, Mali, Morocco, Syria and Tunisia relatively quickly ratified these treaties, but others have hesitated. Within the latter group, Saudi Arabia and Pakistan have, since 1980, been instrumental in developing an alternative set of Islamic Human Rights.

This is due to the fact that the Western human rights doctrine does not fully match the Qur'ānic *Sharī'ah*, which, for example, threatens renegades with legal disadvantages, does not provide for full female legal equality, and does not admit non-Muslims to the highest offices of an Islamic state.

A Muslim legal scholar cannot even ignore the institution of slavery (although it is no longer tolerated anywhere); he has to take into account the fact that the Qur'ān deals with slavery in great detail, discourages the practice, but does not absolutely outlaw it.

The problem of apostasy is simpler, even though renegades were executed at times during the Middle Ages. The Qur'ānic injunction in 5:33 is not read as dealing with peaceful changes of religious affiliation, but rather as intended only for high treason and active conspiracy against an Islamic country. Many modern States foresee the death penalty for such crimes.

Easily defended as well is the exclusion of non-Muslims from the office of *amīr* or *khalīfah*, particularly in view of the complete protection accorded to religious and other minorities under Islamic law. According to the Constitution of the United States, my son Alexander, born an American citizen, cannot become President of the United States because he was born outside the American territory. If this rule is not in violation of human rights, it must equally be acceptable to reserve certain offices to Muslims in an Islamic country.

This brings me to the head-on collision between Western doctrine and Islamic law in the field of female equality. There is no use denying the fact that the *Sharī'ah* presents a counter-model that proceeds from a natural division of roles and functions between the two sexes. On that basis the *Sharī'ah* acts in accordance with the principle that equal treatment is to be accorded only to equal cases and situations, not to unequal ones. Islamic law, at any rate, intends to protect women's dignity and to prevent male exploitation of particular female vulnerabilities rooted in biological differences. The Islamic formula is: equal dignity, different tasks; equal status, different roles; equal value, different capabilities.

There is no way of measuring reliably whether Western career women, as a result of greater "emancipation", enjoy greater fulfilment and happiness than their Oriental sisters. Much speaks against it. I suspect in any event that "quality of life" for women cannot be guaranteed by any "system" but largely results from human attitudes toward other people and toward oneself. Happiness is a matter of the heart.

But one thing must be respected by Western critics: for Muslims, as far as human rights are concerned, God has the last word, and that word is the Qur'ān.

Superstitious numerology

For a Muslim, the Qur'ān is the fixation, in the Arabic language, of God's own communication to mankind. This is the background against which to read the ironical challenge contained in *Sūrah* 11, verse 13: "And so they asserted, 'he (Muḥammad) has invented this'. Say: 'Produce, then, ten *sūrahs* of similar merit, invented by yourselves…'"

It is therefore normal that inquisitive Muslims always tried to unearth a hidden internal structure, an architecture for the Holy Book, just as astronomers attempt to do with the cosmos as a whole. Naturally, this quest was fuelled by the particular desire to penetrate the secret meaning of the so-called *muqaṭṭaʿāt* – enigmatic combinations of up to five letters at the beginning of many *sūrahs*.

Mystical numerology in Islam was a specific technique for clarifying this and other riddles of interpretation. This esoteric and basically cabalistic approach assumes that words, as numerals, can denote or represent certain numbers; it also presumes an occult significance for such numbers.

As proven by the conspicuous absence of the number 13 on hotel doors, this attitude has been quite pervasive outside Islam as well. The Master Cabalist, Papus, described the method in question in plain terms: "Replace letters with numbers, and

vice versa, and carry out arithmetical operations on that basis"
(Die Kabbala, Wiesbaden 1983).

Of course, numerical symbolism, even if presented as
scientific, is pure speculation based on imaginative guesswork
about the "natural" quantitative and qualitative value of the
letters of a given alphabet. In fact, cabalistic theosophy can be
seen as another kind of alchemy: a mathematical sufism,
attempting to obtain magical powers and prophetic insights.

Amazingly, even a Christian theologian recently undertook
such a numerological analysis of the Qur'ān, under the title
Muhammad und Jesus – Die christologisch relevaten Texte des Koran
("Muhammad and Jesus – The Christologically relevant texts
of the Qur'ān", Vienna 1978). The author, Prof. Claus Schedl,
applying a "logo-technical" method, *Cabala* style, for 500 pages
counts, subtracts, and adds digits from left to right, up and
down, only to conclude that:

1. The Qur'ān is well construed;
2. Muḥammad was a creative artist and writer who had
    polished his text until he was satisfied with its artistic
    perfection (p.166);
3. The Qur'ānic Christology is so close to the one in the
    New Testament that a Christian-Muslim dialogue on
    Jesus' mode of acting (not on his status and nature)
    promises to be useful.

In this context, Schedl is honest enough to quote relevant
passages from the Acts of the Apostles (3:13, 26 and 4:27, 30) in
order to remind his readers that the earliest Jewish and Syrian
Christians – in contrast to those of Hellenistic and Latin
background – had seen Jesus exclusively as God's servant (*'abd*).
He even admits that this original Semitic Christianity lives on
within Islam.

It is encouraging that a Christian expert, after having studied the tragic history of the Nestorian church, arrives at this conclusion. But it is discouraging that he does so on the basis of numerological hocus-pocus, and that he reduces the import of Muḥammad through elevating him to the rank of master writer. Allah, He alone, is the architect of the Qur'ān.

Strictly speaking, it is not worthwhile reading beyond page 34 of Schedl's book, where he states: "Since letters also are numbers, we add their respective numerical values." For at that very point, science quits and magic begins.

What arrogance to assume that the Hebrew alphabet not only represents a God-given numerological system but that it also determines the numerology of the Arabic alphabet! Why, may I ask, is *alif* representative of the number 1, *tā* of 400, *rā* of 200 but *hā* only of 5? And who has determined that 55 denotes transcendental perfection, please?

It is amusing to watch these linguistic cabalists at work. One of their tricks is to engage in self-fulfilling prophecies: they alter their methods and criteria for counting until a number of symbolic significance emerges. Such a result is practically assured since the cabalists have loaded virtually every number combination with symbolic value. The following citations help unmask these methods:

- Since there are 86 Makkan *sūrahs*, "the idea imposes itself that numerical symbolism is in play; because 86 is the numerical value of Elohim, the Hebrew name for God" (p.38).
- "It is our guess that they (i.e. the mysterious *muqaṭṭa'āt*) are logo-technical alarm signals securing the text that follows them" (p.205).

Clearly those bent on such speculation never fail to hit a mystical jackpot.

20th century cabalists versed in data processing no doubt are keen on submitting the Qur'ān to computer-supported text analyses. We must therefore brace ourselves for a quantified breakdown of "Muḥammad's style" and even of his preference for particular vowels. That will, in turn, open the door for further micro-electronic games of interpretation confirming the German proverb: the less faith, the more "after-faith".

Is 19 the key?

Brussels, 17 December 1985

Sūrah 74, verse 30, of the Qur'ān rather abruptly states: "Over it are nineteen." Needless to say that many attempts have been undertaken over the centuries to elucidate this strange passage. Does it refer to the angels mentioned in the next verse? Is it a reference to a cosmological numeral, sum total of planets and astrological signs (as Gnostics would be inclined to assume)? Does it denote the nineteen functions of the body that doctors enumerated during the Middle Ages? God alone knows. Or?

Rashid Khalifa, *imām* of the mosque in Tucson, Arizona, tested the role played by the number 19 in the construction of the entire Qur'ān (*Qur'ān: Visual Presentation of the Miracle*, Tucson 1982). In the end, he was able to prove that 19 was a structural element in at least fifty different respects without once reverting to Cabalistic methods. He noticed for instance that:

- The opening formula *(basmalah)* of all but one of the *surahs* consists of 19 consonants;
- The first revelation (96:1–5) was composed of 19 words;
- The Qur'ān possesses 19 x 6 = 114 *sūrahs*;
- God's name, Allah, appears 2698 times in the Qur'ān, a number divisible by 19.

Even more surprising, Rashid Khalifa discovered that the enigmatic opening letters of many *sūrahs*, the *muqaṭṭaʿāt*, themselves invariably reappear in their *sūrahs* in a number that is a multiple of 19. On that basis, the author is of the opinion that he has proven, physically, that the Qur'ān, as it is, is of divine origin. Knowledge can now replace faith.

In fact, Khalifa implies that, via Qur'ānic analysis, he has established what eluded all philosophers before him: a physical proof of God. Not realizing that this logic is circular, he also claims to have ascertained that the Qur'ānic text, as it stands, has never been altered. For would the linguistic and architectural structure, based on 19, not otherwise have suffered?

In my view, Rashid Khalifa's method raises more questions than it can answer:

- Is it axiomatic that verbal revelation possesses numerical structure?
- Could one not find structures in the Qur'ān that are based on other numbers as well, provided one tried equally hard?
- In strictly logical terms, is the structural role played by 19 clear-cut proof that *Sūrah* 74, verse 30, relates to the construction of the Qur'ān, or is it mere coincidence?
- Can we assume that the organization of the Qur'ān (as compared to its revealed content) is in no way a result of human efforts at compilation? Is the separation of *Sūrahs* 113 and 114, for instance, decreed by Allah?

I remain skeptical of all crutches of this sort. When we "testify" that there is God (and none beside Him), we do so precisely because there is no ready proof of a "physical" nature. The truth is, faith is irreplaceable.

Consistency *à la* Küng

Brussels, 15 January 1986

The famous Swiss theologian, Prof. Dr. Hans Küng, now director of an ecumenical research institute in Tübingen (Germany), has been at odds with Catholic orthodoxy for some time. However, with his book, *Christentum und Weltreligionen* ("Christendom and World Religions", 1984), his conflict with Rome reached a new level. Quite sensationally, Küng accepts that Muḥammad was a prophet. In doing so, he continues the work, begun at Marburg University by Prof. Dr. Rudolf Bultmann, of "de-mythologizing" the New Testament. Proceeding logically, Küng includes all the major religions in an "ecumenical dialogue" that was formerly reserved to Christian denominations alone.

During a seminar held at Stuttgart in 1985 on "The Islamic World between Tradition and Progress", Küng pointed out that the Church no longer defended its classical ruling of 1442 that there was no salvation outside its realm (*extra ecclesiam nulla salus*).

From this particular development, and against the overall outcome of the 2nd Vatican Council (1962–1965), Küng concludes that the consequential thesis "*extra ecclesiam nulla propheta*" (no prophets outside the Church) must have become invalid as well. He argues that by recognizing (even if belatedly) that Islam is, and always has been, a genuine path to salvation, the Church can no longer fail to realize that Muḥammad, who is the guide and leader on that path, was a true prophet.

Küng also shares the Muslim view that the New Testament anticipated a further prophet, and that "the prophetic messages of the Bible and the Qur'an undoubtedly agree with each other structurally" (*Zeitschrift fur Kulturaustausch,* 1985/3, pp. 315 ff.).

Küng then coolly asks his angry opponents in the Catholic Church to do their homework on this much neglected world religion. Some Catholic priests already seem to have done this since two of them, from the diocese of Paris, recently embraced Islam.

Notwithstanding those all too few Western intellectuals and artists who have nonetheless discovered Islam – such as the Austrian Leopold Weiss (Muhammad Asad); the British Richard Burton, Marmaduke Pickthall, Martin Lings and Cat Stevens; the French, René Guénon, Eva de Vitray-Meyérovitch, Roger Garaudy and Maurice Béjart – on the whole, Küng's assessment that Westerners know too little about Islam is correct. Even most Western "orientalists" failed to understand Islam in depth. After all, were they not serving mostly colonial interests – consciously or not – when assessing Islam according to the supposedly universal yardstick of Western civilization and its value system?

In the *Muslim World Book Review* (Vol.6, No.1, p.5), Parvez Manzoor quotes Ignaz Goldziher as admitting: "What would be left of the Gospels if the Qur'ānic methods were applied to them?" A meaningful answer to this most relevant question would presuppose a study of the impact on the formulation and interpretation of the New Testament of philosophical and mythological notions existing at that time. This study could include the following:

- The relationship between the Persian sun-god Mithras and his mystery cults and the Latin-Christian *dies soli* and "Sunday" in Christian mythology;
- The relationship between the Egyptian goddess Isis (as "Star of the Sea"/*stella maris* a person of the Egyptian "trinity" of Gods), the Roman mother-goddess Magna Mater (also known as Dea Dia and Kybela), and the Christian cult of Mary, "Mother of God";
- The relationship between the Roman traditions of deifying late emperors through Senate resolutions and the decision of the Council of Nicaea to elevate Jesus to essential godhead in 325.

If historical research is applied to both the sources of religions and their conceptual baggage, Islam has nothing to worry about and Christianity everything. Hans Küng sees this, and proceeds on a path that will eventually lead him to the acceptance of Islam for his own person, God willing.

Popular explosion in Algeria

Algiers, 5–12 October 1988

My memories of the war of independence were so painful that I never intended to touch the Algerian soil again. But then, twenty-five years later, on 17 August 1987, I was made German Ambassador in Algiers.

At first, this beautiful city seemed unchanged, but then the overpopulation and the many symptoms of socialism at work could not be ignored. For instance, living quarters are so scarce that the available apartments are grotesquely overcrowded, and family members are often obliged to use their beds in rotation: the small children during the night, and the older ones – still unemployed – during the day (or at least until their mother throws them all out into the street in order to be able to clean up "home"). No wonder many of these children act like little grown-ups and their faces already bear the marks of old age. When they leave school, there is none of that happy clamour.

The grand idea of industrializing the country from top to bottom – called "*industrialisation industrialisante*" – had not only failed to achieve its aim but had also ruined both agriculture and the crafts. Similarly, virtually all the large industrial complexes, many built in the wrong places, are non-profitable. For instance, the Mitidja Valley around Blida, which was formerly one of the most fertile regions in the country, has become unrecognizable due to too much cement.

After their victory over France, many Algerians believed that they would no longer have to serve anybody, including tourists. But Algeria's natural resources – namely, oil and gas – turned out to be a mixed blessing. Indeed, while these two items accounted for 97% of all revenues from exports, they were barely able to service the public debt and pay for the importation of foodstuffs which Algeria, at an earlier time, had exported. There seemed to be a surplus only in sunshine, sand and children, and people would joke about it, saying that, in a socialist economy, even sand might soon be rationed. Needless to add that the one and only party in power – for a quarter of a century now – monopolized the public, social and economic life, and was not open to any reforms.

Scholarization and medical services, however, had been successful. But this had produced an ever increasing jobless "academic proletariat" that insisted on learning from the "nomenclatura" why a country potentially so rich was in fact so poor. Some of them accused the Communist circles within the *Front de Libération Nationale* (FLN) to have "confiscated" the fruits of the joint Islamic, bourgeois and socialist war effort against France. When these young people spoke of their government, or even of their country, they always referred to "them", never to "us". They were obviously looking for a non-socialist alternative and identity for themselves, both of which could only be provided by their religion: Islam. Indeed, only the mosques offered and constituted a suitable ground for the articulation and organization of protest. Thus a "parallel Islam", next to the official one, was born.

This is the background to the popular uprising that occurred this week, mainly but not only in Algiers. For an entire week, angry teenagers and young men took over, while the police, army and government vanished. The rebels seemed to rampage indiscriminately, but it soon became clear that their real targets were unloved institutions, such as the government, the police, the Party, and even the Polisario. Before the army finally suppressed the uprising by force, the Islamic movement, illegal until now, surfaced as the only force capable of calming the streets and re-establishing order without bloodshed. Thus the *Front Islamique du Salut* (FIS) was born, under the leadership of Abbasi Madani, and it was simultaneously legitimized as an opposition party. It felt in Algiers as one might have felt during the equally short-lived "political spring" of 1968 in Prague.

Shooting continued for some time. However, as I had an armoured Mercedes, I could remain mobile. My main task, besides fact-finding and analyzing the situation, was to prepare the eventual evacuation of the German colony and prevent panic. As is reasonable in such a developing situation, in case of doubt my classical advice was to "stay put". All normal activities having ceased, a skeleton staff would suffice in the Embassy; I therefore left it up to everyone to decide whether it was safe to come to the office. Surprisingly or not, the female secretaries who assured our telex connections with Bonn, seemed to be more courageous, on the whole, than some of their male colleagues...

My wife, too, during these critical hours, did not stop practising her harp. She simply moved into a corner, away from the window, safe from any but ricochet bullets. (Where, may I ask, is such a thing as a "safe" place?)

The last of the 'Ibāḍites

Beni Izguen, 26 May 1989

There is nothing more relaxing in Algeria than to retire to
the M'zab, a stony desert situated 650 kilometres south of
Algiers. It is here, in the middle of nowhere, that the last true
'Ibāḍites found refuge from religious persecution and built seven
incredible cities (such as Ghardaia, Malika, Beni Izguen and
El-Ateuf). It is also here that they cling on, without any
compromise whatsoever, to their rigourist interpretation of
Islam and their Islamic-democratic traditions.

Ethnically Berber but speaking the best Arabic in the
entire country, the Mozabites had participated actively in
the armed struggle against French occupation. In fact, the
headquarters of the southern Wilaya (Military District) of
the FLN forces had been located there. But after the war,
the Mozabites had refused any medals, governmental rents
for veteran guerrilla fighters or other privileges that were
showered on FLN personnel. They had fought for Allah and
His *ummah* alone. They also defended themselves more
successfully than anybody else in the country against
Socialist infiltration.

Via El-Oued and Ouargla – Hassi Messaoud we could not
reach because of a sandstorm – I drove to Beni Izguen. Here
350 men were to listen to my lecture entitled "Ten points I
dislike in the practice of Islam." These points were:

1. The style of preaching used in the Friday sermons (*khuṭba*), namely that preachers usually appeal to emotions more than to the power of reasoning, and that they do so as a general would when calling his troops to battle.

2. The affinity to violence of many young Muslim activists who are prone to enforce their views rather than to rely on conviction – as if one could disregard and omit the "Makkan stage" of winning hearts and minds, and immediately enter the "Madinan stage" of building an Islamic State.

3. The phenomenon of uncritical imitation (*taqlīd*), resulting from the fear of forbidden innovation (*bid'a*), which stands in the way of a rejuvenation of an Islamic jurisprudence relevant to contemporary society.

4. The ethnical arrogance, which could already be found in the attitude of early Muslim peoples (such as the Arabs and the Persians), towards Muslims from other parts of the world. This attitude continues today, in spite of the fact that, according to Muhammad Asad, there are few Muslims but much Islam in the West, whereas there are many Muslims but little Islam in the Muslim world.

5. Islamic history has become the history of despotism, even though the *Sharī'ah* demands government by consent (*shūrā*).

6. Technophobia, or in other words the attitude of rejecting the West lock, stock, and barrel, as if there was such a thing as "Islamic" and "non-Islamic" technology. The *ummah* only had the alternative of mastering modern technology or of being domineered by it.

7. The rigourist, puritanical tendency of turning Islam into an elitist religion, instead of being a religion that is within everyone's reach, by introducing so-called "pious" innovations (*al-bid'a al-ḥasana*).

8. An obsession with marginal issues, which risks turning Islam into a Talmudic religion. What counted was submission to God, and not how one brushes one's teeth.

9. The fractionalization of the Islamic world, which carries pluralism to negative extremes.

10. The marginalization of women, which signifies the marginalization of more than half the Muslim population, incidentally including the mother of every male Muslim.

I did not criticize a lack of tolerance, and rightly so. Instead of running me out of town, these intensely religious men listened to me quietly, respectfully, and skeptically. Many of them belonged to the technical "intelligentsia" of their country.

In the meantime, my wife was spending some time with their women who all grow up and live entirely hidden, veiling themselves totally – except for one eye – when going out.

When my hosts invited me for tea after the lecture, I asked them whether they felt it was not important for an educated husband to have an equally educated wife. The answer was depressingly unequivocal: "How? After all, one does not spend much time with one's wife, or does one?" I was tempted cynically to reply: "Of course, and that in the dark."

On our way back, between Djelfa and Berrouaghia, although there was no storm, we had to drive through 150 kilometres of dense fog, composed of dust particles and impenetrable by our headlights. This means that the desert, jumping over the so-called "green belt" south of the Atlas mountains, is gradually moving towards Algiers, situated only 80 kilometres away. It also proves that nothing can withstand the combined effect of sun, wind, and aridity. But then, the desert grows in people's hearts as well.

Big Bang: no room for God?

Algiers, 22 October 1989

Carl Friedrich von Weizsäcker, the German nuclear scientist, recently affirmed that "the laws of physics do not explain what 'matter' really is. These laws only inform us about how our perception must be constructed for us to encounter objects." This was a fundamental discovery both in macro and microphysics. Indeed, ever since Werner Heisenberg enunciated in 1927 the principle of uncertainty or indeterminacy (*Unschärferelation*), originally with regard to the position and velocity of the electron, we have been cautioned against taking as reality what, in fact, is only the result of a specific method of inquiry.

Nevertheless, cosmologues (such as Stephen Hawking) compete with each other in explaining the physical origin of the universe. Thanks to Albert Einstein's theory of relativity, the so-called "Big Bang theory" has gained credibility because we are now used to assume that time is a dimension of space, and space a dimension of time. This assumption also allows the speculation that before the coming into being of the cosmos there was no space (and therefore no time) and no time (and therefore no space).

Philosophers have always maintained that God created the world *ex nihilo*, namely, from nothing – nothing implying no space *and* no time. But classical philosophers never denied that the world was created nor did they affirm that it was the result of a mindless process. Maybe Stephen Hawking should be asked from where the potential, the conditions and the matter for a "big bang" could have come?

Natural scientists need only to move back by a link or two along the causal chain – the very chain that eventually leads back to Allah, the Creator and Maintainer of all the worlds.

"When the earth trembles…"

Algiers, 29 October 1989

Today was the Turkish national holiday. As we drove to my Turkish colleague's reception, on a very sultry evening, we noticed that all our cats had disappeared – a bad omen in this earthquake-prone place. Then, on our way back, we were alarmed to see that people had left their houses, many holding babies in their arms. Only then did we realize that, once more, Algiers had started to shake.

We, too, stayed outside, frightened and unsteady on our feet when the palm trees started dancing. Most frightening, though, was the noise: a roaring sound as if a train was about to run us over. In fact, the epicentre was some 60 kilometres away, as usual in the coastal area near Tipasa.

And yet, a Muslim should not panic when encountering such unimaginably powerful natural forces, no matter how helpless and dwarfed one may feel during such a strong earthquake (6° on the Richter scale). Rather, one should think of what awaits us in the future, as is described in the 99th *sūrah* of the Qur'ān, *al-Zalzalah*, which describes how the Day of Judgment will begin: exactly like today, only much worse, with an earthquake of gigantic proportions.

The *sūrah* ends as follows: "Then, whoever has done an atom's weight of good, will see it; and whoever has done an atom's weight of evil, will see it."

Islam: The Alternative

Taroudant, 24 April 1991

From the United States comes the unlikely news that Francis Fukuyama, Head of the Policy Planning Staff of the State Department, has proclaimed the "end of history". The demise of world Communism obviously made him draw the fantastic conclusion that the "American way of life" was bound to become universal. With the "Second World" out of the way, the underdeveloped "Third World" could not but accept the "First World" as its obligatory model. That is what might be called triumphalism at its best (or worst).

Following a good custom of the German Foreign Service, we are spending our first holiday within our host country, Morocco. Our Volkswagen Golf is taking us on an exotic round trip, starting in the ski resort (!) of Ifrane, south of Fes, via the Middle and High Atlas mountain ranges to El-Rashidiya, Erfoudh, Rissani, Tinghirt, Ouazazate and Agadir, all the way to Tiznit on the edge of the Western Sahara.

In the historical hotel, Palais Salam of Taroudant, capital of the (if it rains) fertile Sousse region, I suddenly realize that I should answer Fukuyama's statement by pointing out that the East-West conflict had simply been replaced by a North-South one – symptom of the fact that there still exists an alternative to the Western way of life, namely, Islam. In doing so, I should try to defuse the many major prejudices against Islam, which are so deeply anchored in the Western psyche, devoting a chapter each to issues such as holy war, fatalism, obscurantism, intolerance, the *ḥijāb* and Islamic penal law.

The next day we returned to Rabat prematurely so that I could start organizing the book and formulating my ideas. Twenty-three days later, the manuscript was ready, except for the index. And finally two months after that, the prestigious Eugen Diederichs Publishing House in Munich took the book into its autumn programme. It was called *Islam: The Alternative.*[3]

---

3. 1992; 4th ed. Munich 1999. English edition: 3rd ed. Amana Publications, Belteville, MD, 1999.

The oldest city in the world?

Damascus, 10 February 1992

L ike Aleppo and Jericho, Damascus, too, claims to be the oldest city in the world. Yet Damascus, the intellectual capital of the Near East, definitely has more to offer than perpetuity. The Arabic spoken here is so distinct, nuanced and beautiful that Rainer Maria Rilke, the German master of musical poetry, was taken over by it without any need for comprehension. However, one thing that is indisputable, is that the area between the Euphrates, the Tigris and the Mediterranean Sea was a cultural cradle of humanity. (For verification, a visit to the local national museum suffices.)

The *via recta*, a straight road, 2 km long, that cuts through the old town, is still there, as described in the Acts of the Apostles. The city is also a reminder of St. Paul who converted to Christianity nearby in 33 CE, and later, with his extremist Christology, became the real founder of Christendom.

Damascus is one of those places described in the Michelin Guide as "*vaut le voyage*" (worth the trip). But I came here for one single reason: in order to pray in the marvellous Umayyad mosque. Friday mosque for the fourteen Umayyad caliphs who resided here until 750, it is, after the Great Mosques of Makkah and Madinah, the Dome of the Rock and the Aqsa Mosque in Jerusalem, certainly the fifth most revered jewel of the Islamic architectural heritage. Its coloured mosaics that depict plants but also contemporary urban architecture are part of the cultural heritage of all mankind.

Since the dynasty's only survivor (after the Abbasid revolt) founded the Andalusian caliphate in Cordoba, one cannot either unravel its history without returning, sooner or later, to Damascus. The extraordinary Kurdish Prince Ṣalāḥ al-Dīn (Saladin), who was the Crusaders' greatest opponent and a legend even during his lifetime, also lived in Damascus for ten years and is buried just outside the Great Damascene Mosque. The fact that John the Baptist is buried inside it is an anomaly rooted in the Christian past of the building. This mosque has, however, not only a past but also a future: according to a certain Islamic eschatology, at the end of time, Jesus is to return here, more precisely on the south-eastern minaret...

Today, the temperature outside is a freezing minus 5°C, and as we approach Damascus airport we witness a spectacle as grandiose as it is absurd: the sand dunes are covered with snow, and so too is the Umayyad mosque. In fact, the ground is so slippery that on my way to prayer I am on all fours!

The next day, I visit the tomb of Muḥy al-Dīn Ibn al-'Arabī, the Andalusian *Shaykh al-Akbar* who died here in 1240 and is considered the greatest of all Sufi masters, even by some Christian mystics. The area in which his grave is located, on the northern edge of the city, strikes one as so Ottoman in spirit that it could have been transported here from Istanbul. It is a theosophical island of peace.

For me, there is no doubt that Ibn 'Arabī's gnostic illumination is unverified and unverifiable, and that he more than just brushed against pantheism – as a logical outcome of his neo-Platonic doctrine of *waḥdat al-wujūd* (the unity of all being). Whether the Qur'ān for Ibn 'Arabī was text or pretext, who is to say?

I do not deny the intellectual justification, but the answerability of the question as to whether God is immanent or transcendent, whether He is One or All. A Muslim should, however, avoid giving exclusive or conclusive answers to such questions, being confident that "God is closer to us than our jugular vein" and simultaneously, that He is the Unfathomable. Any other approach risks producing a theomorphic doctrine of man, which is as bad as a pan-anthropomorphic image of God.

At night, from my hotel room I see illuminated crosses on church steeples all over the old town. This makes me think of the many minarets in the United States and in Europe from which it is forbidden to call for prayer.

Summary execution
by the media

Rabat, 15 March–8 April 1992

In early 1992, the Eugen Diederichs Publishing House in Munich pre-announced *Islam: The Alternative* to bookshops and the media. This immediately provoked resistance, well before the book appeared, even among travelling book salesmen.

Fuelled by leftist feminists, I could now read in the German press that I advocated polygamy, the stoning of adulterers, and the beating-up of women – all inaccurate accusations made up out of the blue – and was therefore most unfit to be the Ambassador of a Christian country. (Which one?) Even in Parliament, members of the Social-Democrat Party started discussing whether I should be recalled.

My main defence problem was that the book with which I could have refuted all these silly accusations did not become available until April 6th, namely three weeks after the media campaign began to unfold.

I could now also read that I had supposedly driven a member of my Embassy staff to suicide, and that I had forced my entire female staff in Rabat to veil themselves. Serious accusations, even if they were mere fabrications.

As Information Director of NATO from 1983 to 1987, I had been a media man myself, dealing with many journalists specialized in issues of military defence and nuclear strategy. Since they were an international elite, I remained perhaps innocent of the potential "yellow journalism" that I am now experiencing in Germany.

Against the background of the on-going defamation of Islam in the context of both the Rushdie affair and the Gulf War, some TV and print media (especially the tabloid *Bild am Sonntag*) are clearly out to prove, with me as the victim, that Islam is unconstitutional, thereby drawing a line between a majority of good and a minority of bad people, the Muslims. In German, this (basically fascist) method is called "*ausgrenzen*" (out-fencing), and the media involved are labelled as "*Hinrichtungsmedien*" (execution media).

It would be easy to "prove" with the same method (but with more justification) that Judaism and Christianity are also "unconstitutional". It is, after all, not the Qur'ān but the Bible that calls for the stoning of adulterers, and it is not the Qur'ān but the New Testament that contains revolting passages denigrating women.

The media attacks have become so vicious that I am beginning to feel like an outlaw. Of course, the Foreign Office in Bonn could not allow me, its ambassador, to conduct my own media defence, nor could it intervene on my behalf until very recently when the alleged *corpus delicti* became available on the market. A catch 22 situation if there ever was one.

When the Foreign Office was finally able to read *Islam: The Alternative* thanks to an advance copy hastily scrapped together, the book was found to be objective and unobjectionable. I was "cleared" through a press release – which the media, of course, did not care to diffuse – and continued my job as ambassador to the Kingdom of Morocco.

No excuses were made, nor did anybody assess the grief caused to members of my family. I, as a matter of fact, had probably suffered the least because the entire campaign had occurred during the month of Ramaḍān, and the fasting had helped me to keep an even greater distance than normal from matters of secondary importance, such as career and prestige.

For the Muslim community in Germany, however, the incident was and will remain highly significant. Indeed, it was a clear attempt to put Muslims in their place, not to mention the media verdict that they are pursuing something, namely Islam, that is "politically incorrect". Could it be that Germans, no longer allowed to indulge in anti-Jewish anti-Semitism, are now beginning to indulge in anti-Arab anti-Semitism, and that the Muslims, on both religious and ethnical grounds, are becoming new scapegoats?

Evening lessons

Rabat, 19 March 1992

Year after year, evening after evening, during most of the month of Ramaḍān, I sit crouched on the floor of the Royal Palace of Rabat, listening for a couple of hours – until just before *ifṭār* – to what professors of theology from the entire Islamic world have to say. And so do the complete Moroccan cabinet, the general staff of the Moroccan armed forces, and the entire Muslim *corps diplomatique* accredited here. In fact, as the event is being televised, the entire nation is spending the last hours before the breaking of the fast together.

Until King Hassan II and the princes arrive, there is highly accomplished Qur'ān recitation, frequently by mere boys from Southeast Asia. The word of God, presented so artfully and powerfully, is spellbinding whether one understands its meaning or not.

The individual speakers, however, one ought to understand, even if they do not always address the most relevant of topics from their high chair. But that depends, in my case, on whether they express themselves in classical Arabic (*al-fuṣḥā*), as is normal for scholars from Palestine, Lebanon, Jordan and Syria, or slide into their local dialects, as the North Africans are wont to do. My Syrian Arab teacher put it succinctly: "Qur'ānic Arabic is only recited; classical

Arabic is only written; and colloquial Arabic is only spoken." Nevertheless, it is a unique feat of the Arabic language to have remained as it was some 1400 years ago, the vocabulary of the Qur'ān having become vernacular. We, in contrast, cannot even read Chaucer without help.

The arrangement of these lectures, called "*Al-Durūs al-Ḥasaniyya*", is symbolic. Like us, the king sits on the floor, listening and looking up to the *ustādh* on the high chair. Thus wisdom is symbolically placed above power. While sitting there, we are travelling back into the history of Islamic teaching – to the Azhar University in Cairo, the Zeytuna in Tunis, the Qarawiyin in Fes. Indeed, just as now, the students would sit on the floor, surrounding their teacher who would lean against a column in the mosque and expound a legal problem by addressing it first on the basis of the Qur'ān, secondly by drawing on the *Sunnah* of the Prophet, and finally by finding analogies to these two sources of Islamic jurisprudence.

It does happen that the king intervenes – as he did when he asked the Great Muftī of Egypt, Muḥammad al-Ṭanṭāwī (now Great Shaykh of al-Azhar), not to shorten his exposition but to expand on it by coming back the next day.

After these lectures, the Muslim ambassadors, taking turns, invite many of the participants for *ifṭār*-dinner in their residences. Today it was my turn. After sunset, we served water, juice, almond milk and a few dates; then we prayed the evening prayer (*ṣalāt al-maghrib*) all together on the garden terrace. The highly esteemed secretary general of the historic Istiqlal Party, Maître Muhammad Boucetta, accepted to be our *imām*.

The dinner, including *shorba frique* – the obligatory heavy Ramaḍān soup – roast lamb (*mashwī*) and, for dessert, *baklava* and *muhallabiyya*, was eaten so fast that everybody was home with his family before the night prayer (*ṣalāt al-'ishā'*).

Will there ever be a time, I wonder, when it will be normal for ministers, royal counsellors, and party leaders to come to the residence of a German ambassador for prayer? (Since I am a Muslim, I am not allowed to make a bet, nor am I required to disclose what bet I would have made!)

Pilgrimage as a logistical problem

Rabat, April 1992

It is old German military wisdom that every problem can be reduced to logistics, thereby becoming manageable. In case of *ḥajj*, some of these problems are: inoculation against meningitis; obtaining a pilgrim's visa from the Saudi Embassy; and booking a flight (in competition with 50,000 Moroccans trying to do the same).

One also needs to equip oneself with the specific pilgrim's outfit: two pieces of unsewn white cotton material of equal size (1 x 1.8 metres); a pair of unsewn sandals; an unsewn leather belt with three compartments (for identification papers and tickets, medicaments, and cash); a possibly life-saving white umbrella, and an unsewn sack (for carrying a copy of the Qur'ān, a notebook, a reserve can of Pepsi Cola, and some dried food). Our doctor, well acquainted with the health problems encountered by pilgrims, suggests we take along something against fever, headache, nausea, diarrhea, and sore feet.

But all this is only the physical baggage. As performing the pilgrimage is a religious endeavour one must acquaint oneself with its spiritual aspects and antecedents, many dating back to the traditions of Abrahamic monotheism. Otherwise one risks being overwhelmed by the stress and strain caused by an extremely tough climate and the great concentration of people. I therefore read all I can and ask a thousand questions of friends who have already been on *hajj*. I so much want to go – my life feels incomplete without it. And yet I am somehow afraid.

Matters are not improved by the fact that friends and neighbours have started to pay me the customary "goodbye visits". Indeed, here in Morocco, people recall very vividly how dangerous the 12,000 kilometre trip to and from Makkah used to be: before the jet age, it took about a year, and frequently it was a trip without return.

Patient in adversity

Muhammad V Airport, Casablanca, 28 May 1992

All evening and through the entire night we wait in vain for the Saudi jumbo to arrive. But as is expected from and mandatory for a pilgrim: nobody complains; nobody files a protest. Rather, we huddle together, praying the night prayer and the early morning prayer on hard marble floors.

Finally at 5.37 am, with a ten hour delay, we depart for Jeddah. Instead of the usual music, we are comforted by Qur'ānic recitation coming through the loudspeaker.

My seat neighbours are Muslims from Senegal – the most pious of the pious. Among them is an admirable lad, Mokhtar Diouri, one of the sons of President Diouf.

Before we enter the wider airspace of Makkah, the captain reminds us that it is time to restate our intention (*niyya*) to perform *ḥajj*, put on the pilgrim's garb and, if only in a sitting position, pray two *rak'ah*. In no time, the entire passenger's cabin turns white.

In the Prophet's garden

Enlarged time and again, the Prophet's Mosque in *al-Madīnah al-munauwara* (the enlightened city) no longer, as in 1982, only covers a block of the city; it now extends over an entire area. Currently surrounded by eleven minarets (fourteen are planned), the mosque allows 480,000 people to pray simultaneously. In spite of being open on the sides and partially without a ceiling, temperatures are relatively moderate. A German Muslim engineering firm near Stuttgart ingeniously constructed giant light-metal umbrellas that turn towards the sun during daytime and fold at night, while cold water circulates under the floor.

When, at prayer time, hundreds of thousands of pilgrims and non-pilgrims converged, Shaykh Nahnah of Algeria and I also approached the mosque, not on foot but in an air-conditioned limousine. Believe it or not: everybody gave way, peacefully, without sneering or hammering on the roof – as would have happened in any other circumstances. Religious fervour belied the laws of mass sociology!

In the mosque, my neighbours were a Pakistani banker from Bahrain and a Turkish guest worker from Bochum, Germany. The three of us, *in nuce*, thus manifesting the universality of Islam.

Only around midnight, the mosque having emptied a bit, did we have a chance to visit its small historical section, *al-*

Rawḍa, the Prophet's garden, which, during his time, was surrounded with the quarters of his wives. It is exactly there, in 'Ā'ishah's room, that Muḥammad is buried, with both his lieutenants, Abū Bakr and 'Umar. Here, where the beloved Prophet lived, worked, preached, made love, and died, many of my co-pilgrims, sobbing and weeping, seemed to lose themselves completely. Had they not dreamed for years of coming so close to the man whose mission had changed their lives?

In contrast to 1982, the Prophet's Mosque now borders the historical burial grounds of al-Baqī'. Not only that, but the cemetery where so many members of his family and Companions are buried (including 'Uthmān, Fāṭimah and 'Ā'ishah) has now been levelled in such a way that, except for experts, individual graves can no longer be recognized. A radical way indeed to forestall hero-worshipping and sanctification! Shaykh Nahnah and I saw how anger about this state of affairs was beginning to boil up among a large group of Iranian pilgrims. But no explosion occurred. Peacefulness and patience being the cardinal characteristics of a *ḥājjī*, any turmoil would have invalidated their pilgrimage.

The Saudis are just as radical in their unsentimental Wahhābī approach to their architectural heritage – tiny as it is – which includes the mosque in Qubā and the Qiblatayn mosque. In 1982, my wife and I had still found them intact. But both have since been replaced by larger modern structures. What a stunning sense of priorities!

After the night prayer, Shaykh Nahnah and I spent hours talking with Algerian students. Can anyone guess what the subject might have been?

Ḥajj is not 'umrah

E ver since I first set (my right) foot in the magnificent Great
Mosque of *Makkah al-mukarrama* (the most noble Makkah),
I have suffered from nostalgia for it. I am constantly homesick
for the atmosphere reigning there, where God is totally in focus.
(To compare it to any Christian place of pilgrimage would be
utterly misleading. Makkah is unique.)

This time we reached the Ḥaram through one of the many
new traffic tunnels that have been dug through the rocky hills
surrounding Makkah, making them look as if they were made
of Swiss cheese. We surfaced immediately in front of the
"mosque of all mosques". A beautiful shock: the overwhelming
feeling of being suddenly transported home.

So, once more, I circumambulated the Ka'bah seven times
and, once more, I rushed between the (stylized) hilltops of Ṣafā
and Marwah. However, the difference this time, is that it is not
winter but summer (with an average temperature of 44°C),
and that I am not one in ten thousand but one in two million
pilgrims.

The crowd is so packed that it is impossible to protect oneself
against the cruel sun with an umbrella. This is a critical situation
because during *ḥajj* it takes about two hours to fulfil the ritual
requirements of *ṭawāf* and *sa'y*. At times, I could not even control
my movements, becoming like a drop of water in an enormous

human wave, undulating to and fro. Now I was glad that I had already been able to acquaint myself with the sites during *'umrah*. However, with such physical effort, it was difficult to remain conscious of the spiritual dimensions of what the others and I were doing.

Next time around, I tried to escape the crowd by walking around the Ka'bah on the second floor, which is on the roof of the mosque's enclosure, even if this meant that the distance to be covered was considerably longer. But, up there, the floor was boiling hot. After reacting like a dancing bear for a little while, I had to abandon my plan.

Under such conditions and with such a large pilgrim population it is no surprise that there are casualties, particularly from sunstroke and circulatory collapse. After each and every ritual prayer we pronounce the "prayer for the dead" for the pilgrims deceased since the last prayer. There is every chance (not risk) that I will be among them.

While circling the Ka'bah, recalibrating myself and retuning myself *vis-à-vis* God, I pray: "O Allah, see to it that your objective reality becomes my subjective reality: a reality felt by myself at any time, anywhere." This private prayer (*du'ā'*) has become the *leitmotiv* of my *ḥajj*.

'Arafāt

On the eve of the all-decisive "Day of 'Arafāt", all pilgrims are tense, for their presence at 'Arafāt (*al-wuqūf*) is a *conditio sine qua non* of *ḥajj*. No 'Arafāt, no *ḥajj*. No wonder everyone is a bit nervous. Allah, please, no last minute hitch!

At last, there we all are, more than two million people clad in what looks like their shrouds, anticipating the Day of Judgment, calling out: "*Labbayk Allāhumma, labbayk!*" (Here I am, O Allah, at Your disposal!). Who in the West is still capable of grasping such intensity of worship and devotion?

In the late afternoon, the very sermon that Muḥammad delivered exactly here from Mount 'Arafāt during his last pilgrimage in 632 is read out. I share my little tent with an American Muslim, professor of economic statistics at Georgetown University. We pray, contemplate, pray, discuss, and pray, hour after hour.

It is so hot (52°C) that the air has begun to vibrate. During my short trip to the nearby toilet, without my umbrella, my feet are burned. But I do not notice it. Experienced pilgrims know: during *ḥajj* even major hardships appear like minor nuisances.

After sunset, 50,000 buses try to leave for, and reach, Muzdalifa simultaneously. The result is a traffic jam worthy of the Guinness Book of Records. Muzdalifah, where we are to stop for the evening prayer (*ṣalāt al-maghrib*), is only seven kilometres away, but it takes us four hours to get there. We should have been totally exhausted, hungry and thirsty. Instead we perform both the evening and night prayers together, collect the correct number of pebbles (for "stoning the Devil"), and rush on to Minā. There, in the middle of the night, we perform this ancient ritual, symbolizing our personal rejection of all that is evil. Then, before we know it, we are back in Makkah for the morning prayer, only just making it before sunrise.

Tired beyond description and happy, also beyond description, we perform our near to last *ṭawāf*, belatedly realizing that we have become *Ḥujjāj*, true pilgrims. I take a long look at the Ka'bah, this temple of unqualified monotheism, which has achieved its architectural perfection not through complexity but through utmost simplicity.

After twenty-six hours on our feet, in this climate, we reach our interim hotel for the next three days in Minā, congratulating each other and asking Allah to accept our pilgrimage. When I woke up, it was already evening and time for the second stoning ritual.

The Feast of Sacrifice – right then and there

Minā, 11–12 June 1992

Today, Muslims around the world are celebrating *ʿĪd al-Aḍḥā* (the feast of sacrifice) in imitation of what is happening right here, where some 10,000 butchers from the entire Muslim world will slaughter about 500,000 sheep in and around Minā. Most of the meat, immediately frozen, will be shipped as of tomorrow to needy regions in the Muslim world, such as Somalia. When I paid for my lamb, I gave instructions for its meat to be flown to Bosnia.

This animal sacrifice, too, is highly symbolic. It is performed in commemoration of Abraham's readiness to sacrifice his son Ismael – if God so willed – and of Ismael's readiness to be sacrificed – if God so willed. God, however, did not wish this to happen, and thus abolished once and for all the horrible custom of sacrificing human beings. Abraham's and Ismael's submission to God having been tested, a ram was sacrificed instead. Thus, we pilgrims are to recall that we must always be willing to forego what is most dear to us if it becomes incompatible with our submission to God. Only then are we immune against worshipping modern idols.

On my way to performing the stoning ritual for the third and last time, I was crossing Minā in the middle of the night. Everywhere people were sleeping in the street, and many buses kept their engines running in order to provide climatization to their occupants. Their exhaust fumes and the stench of food waste was such that I had to protect my nose with a cloth drenched in Eau de Cologne.

In that not very normal situation, and as if everybody would know Turkish, a Turkish pilgrim addressed me with the disarming question: "*Şeytan nerede?*" (Where is the Devil?) Instead of bursting out in laughter, I soberly showed him the approach to the closest of the three pillars that symbolize Satan. It is not every day that one can locate the Devil so concretely, or is it?

On the second day of the festival, King Fahd b. 'Abd al-'Azīz invited me to lunch in his Minā residence. Among the other guests I noticed the Sultan of Brunei, a son of the Iranian President Rafsanjani, a Pakistani chief justice, and Anis Mansour, the prolific Egyptian writer. This was a reminder of the important fact that the pilgrimage to Makkah is also, year after year, an informal intellectual and political summit meeting and a mobile university.

The royal lunch followed Islamic etiquette: to talk extensively before the meal, to speak little (and eat fast) at the table, and to leave the moment one has finished eating. Thus, contrary to the Western custom, I did not wait for the king "to lift the table". Rather I left when I had eaten enough. This is a method that leaves even a king alone at his table, after his last guest has taken his leave.

When I flew back to Rabat from Jeddah a few days later, the steward handed me the latest copy of *Time Magazine*. The headline on the cover read: "Islam: should the world be afraid?"

If only they were whales...

In the Foreign Office, I run into my very old and very good friend Dr. Hansjörg Eiff, Germany's last Ambassador to Yugoslavia (before it broke up). We are both depressed because, for two years now, the so-called civilized world, supposedly representing humanism and concerned for human rights, has been almost passively watching Bosnia being destroyed and its Muslim population massacred.

In my view, the entire tragedy could have been prevented if some of the NATO countries had interfered decisively and in time, according to the rules of crisis management and escalation domination so often practised during staff exercises. The aggressor could have been isolated and, at very short notice, threatened with disadvantages unacceptable to him because they would far outweigh possible gains from his aggression.

The opposite happened. It was not Serbia that was isolated through an effective embargo, but Bosnia. The deadlines attached to threats were so long that Belgrade was indirectly signalled that it need not worry. If anybody was deterred, it was the Western countries, victims of self-deterrence. Instead of leaving Serbian generals in some doubt, Western military "experts" reassured them almost daily by proclaiming that a military solution in the Balkans was not possible, or would be too costly and counter-productive.

Against this background, Western humanitarian aid looked like an alibi. The West was making sure that the Bosnians were not hungry when they were massacred. As an American senator put it: "If only the Bosnians were whales, they might at least have had Greenpeace and the International Wildlife Fund on their side."

How is this horrendous failure of public moral to be explained? Why was there no public outcry against the failure of governments to act? I can only think of two coherent explanations. The first is drawn from the fact that failure to draw practical conclusions from correct insight is a typical symptom of decadence. Could the moral decline of the West have reached a stage where any sacrifice without material gain is no longer sustainable in a crass materialistic and hedonist society? Muslims suspected that the West has *de facto* been de-christianized; now they know.

The second explanation is directly related to the fact that the victims were Muslims. Like many Western observers, I am deeply convinced that NATO countries would have immediately and decisively intervened if the Serbs had been Muslims and the Bosnians Catholics or Jews. (It would of course have helped if, in addition, there had been oil and natural gas fields in Bosnia and Herzegovina.) Hardly anybody will admit it, but it is only thinly disguised: many European politicians would have felt quite uncomfortable with an Islamic state in the centre of their continent. They need not worry: the Dayton Agreement assures that this cannot become a reality.

The Bosnian Muslims are the first but probably not the last victims in Europe of an unfolding campaign of hate, misinformation and defamation against all things Islamic. What the media sow from their desks can become bloody reality in the streets.

But damage has also been done on the other side of the cultural divide. What will be the long-term consequences in the Muslim world of the cynicism developing there about Western style "human rights" and "democracy"? Too many Muslim youths, in the Arab world in general and in Palestine in particular, can see right through the double standards in Western foreign policy, last but not least comparing how democracy fared in Haiti as compared to Algeria.

These developments are the very opposite to bridge building and make a clash of civilizations look like a self-fulfilling prophecy after all.

What a thing to be ashamed of!

Munich, 22 July 1993

Today we celebrated the 20th anniversary of the Mosque in Munich-Freimann whose very soul is Ahmad von Denffer. Qur'ān recitation, historical reminiscences, congratulatory telegrams, speeches.

One intervention, made by the representative of the Lutheran Church, Superior Counsellor Klautke, stirred everyone. He said: "I feel very much at home with you in this mosque because in this environment it is absolutely natural to speak about God. In my own church, at times, I have the impression that people shy away from referring to Him, as if they were ashamed."

If it has really come to this – that to be a Christian is no more than a humanitarian feeling – Islam, with its undamaged transcendental links, is indeed the only alternative for a spiritual reconstruction of Europe.

How to be politically correct

Frankfurt, 15 October 1995

It is quite clear by now: Salman Rushdie can publish whatever he wishes. To criticize him is taboo. On the other hand, somebody writing about Islam with any noticeable degree of sympathy might find himself in deep trouble.

That is what Annemarie Schimmel, the world famous German expert on Sufism, learned this autumn, shortly after she had been nominated for the prestigious annual prize of the German Booksellers' Union. When the media descended upon her, she confessed – without in the slightest justifying Khomeini's famous anti-Rushdie *fatwā* – that she had been personally shocked and grieved, like millions of Muslims, by the blasphemies contained in *The Satanic Verses*.

That did it. From having been an object of media interest, she was now targeted as their pet victim. Her books, many dozens of them, were screened for offensive views, in vain. The only thing this professor of Islamic studies (both in Harvard and Bonn) could be reproached for was that she had pursued her Islamic research with empathy rather than with disgust.

Like others of her friends, I tried to persuade Mrs. Schimmel not to withdraw, for otherwise the damage done to Islam in Germany would be immeasurable. The German President, Roman Herzog, shared this view. When he announced that he would personally hand the prize to her, as planned, the matter was clinched.

Today, transmitted by radio and TV, President Herzog handed the prize to Annemarie Schimmel. In their speeches, both of them said many wonderful things about Islam as a religion and a civilization, and warned of the danger of laicism becoming an intolerant pseudo-religion, thus wielding the weapon of "political correctness".

A battle won for Islam, and for freedom of speech.

Dialogue or confrontation

Cairo, 24–27 July 1996

As in 1993 and 1995, I am participating in the annual international conference of the Egyptian Supreme Islamic Council. However, I no longer represent just myself, but also the Central Council of Muslims in Germany (ZMD), which was created in 1995 as, hopefully, the authentic umbrella organization of Islam in my country. This year, ex-Chancellor Helmut Schmitt participates, confessing that it was the late President Anwar Sadat who had introduced him to the strength and beauties of Islam during a Nile cruise.

Yet, even without such stars of wisdom (including the Copt Pope, Shanuda II), the conference would be worthwhile, if only for the many Muslims from around the globe that one can come to know. For instance, the much revered Shaykh Sabri Kotchi from Albania, who had to spend twenty-seven years in Communist prisons for being a Muslim; or Mufti Yakub Efendi Slumic from Sarajevo, who virtually radiates *baraka*; or many other Muslims from Korea, China, Japan, Argentina, Brazil, Moscow, Kiev, Alma Ata, Lagos, Nairobi…

Of course, the chance of meaningful exchanges around the conference table diminishes with every additional participant. (That is why, content and research-wise, I prefer smaller conferences, such as the ones held by the Jordanian Royal Academy in Amman every other year.)

One thing seems to be typical of Islamic conferences from Rabat to Riyadh: they tend to unite representatives of the status quo, be it government officials or *'ulamā'*. Yet, does it really make sense to discuss the need for dialogue and tolerance – whether dealing with the North-South relationship or the situation in Muslim countries – in the absence of those who challenge the status quo as being unjust, undemocratic, and un-Islamic? Of course, it is always easier to speak *about* one's opponents than *with* them. Yet, this way, fear and frustration are bound to continue, and security, instead of being guaranteed by consent, will continue to be upheld by the police.

During the official ceremony on the occasion of the Prophet's birthday (*mawlūd al-nabī*), President Hosni Mubarak handed to Prof. Annemarie Schimmel and me the Order of the Nile, 1st class, in recognition of what we have been able to do for the renaissance of Islam. We interpret this decoration, however, as also being a gesture against anti-Islamic circles in Europe.

After Malcolm X

For the second year in a row, I have been on a lecture tour in the United States. Last year, except for the Washington area, I mainly participated in the impressive annual conference of the Islamic Society in North America (Columbus, Ohio, 30 August–2 September). This year, it was a coast-to-coast tour organized and sponsored by the Santa Clara and Washington based Council on American-Islamic Relations (CAIR), a very effective and dedicated Muslim civil rights organization.

To have seen Muslims at work in Washington itself – American Muslim Council (AMC); the International Institute of Islamic Thought at Herndon, VA, and its American Graduate School for Islamic and Social Sciences at Leesburg, VA; the Institute of Islamic and Arabic Sciences in America (IIASA) in Fairfax, VA – is one thing; to see American Islam in the provinces, is quite another. This year, I was exposed to Muslim life in Santa Clara, Anaheim, and Los Angeles, CA; Phoenix, Arizona; Detroit, Dearborn, Chicago, Milwaukee, Lansing, and Patterson, New Jersey, and that made me even more optimistic than I already was.

On the whole, in comparison to Islam in Europe, I see six major differences favouring the development of Islam in America:

1. As there is a very large non-immigrant Islamic community in the US, nobody can say, for example to the Afro-American Muslims, "Why don't you go back to where you came from?" – as foreign Muslims are frequently told in Europe.

2. Although there are many Muslim immigrants in the US (except in Dearborn with its dense Lebanese Shī'ī population), there is no dominating ethnic group. In Europe, in contrast, most Muslims in France are North Africans, in the United Kingdom are Indo-Pakistanis, and in Germany are Turks. The American scene is consequently less subject to massive ethnic prejudice or a fear of cultural submersion.

3. Many immigrant American Muslims and their children are academically trained, well-earning, and respected citizens, whereas in Europe, most immigrant Muslims enter the country as guest workers and are unskilled labour.

4. America has always been multi-religious, Europe not.

5. Europeans suffer from collective memories that go back to the Crusades and the Ottoman campaigns into Central Europe. Europe also borders on Muslim countries: to the south, North Africa, and to the east, Turkey and Central Asia. This causes mutual fears and anxieties that the average American is spared.

6. Most American Muslims are American citizens, which is not the case in Europe. And without citizenship, a Muslim can hardly be assertive.

I should add another point: American Muslims are Americans, which is to say that they are more or less as dynamic, innovative, technology-conscious, aggressive, and well-organized as Americans generally are.

Of course, not everything is rosy over there. I am not worried about the heterodox Nation of Islam, for just as many former members of the Black Muslims, including Muhammad 'Ali and Malcolm X, finally saw the light, others will too. Sooner or later, Sunnī Islam will also prevail among Afro-Americans. What worries me more is the lack of sufficient integration between Black and White communities at the mosque level. If this continues with the third generation of immigrants, there must be something structurally wrong.

Finally, American Muslims have to put up with a formidable "born adversary": extremely skilled and powerful Zionist media and pressure groups, which are not as influential or as present in Europe. As long as the Jewish lobby continues to believe that Israel is better off whenever Islam fares worse, our religion will be in an uphill battle. But uphill battles can also be won.

Muslim of the Year

Los Angeles, 3 October 1998

I have come to southern California for just one day in order to receive the annual prize given by the Islamic Information Service for the "Muslim of the Year". Like so many immigrant Muslim academic professionals in America, Dr. Nazir U. Khaja, M.D., an urologist of Indian origin graduated from Harvard Medical School, devotes an extraordinary amount of his time to Islamic *da'wah*. The films and videos he and Farouk Ubaysi produce in Altadena by interviewing personalities such as Muhammad Asad and Annemarie Schimmel find distribution all over the Muslim world. What prompted him to make me a recipient of his prize is probably the popularity among American Muslims of a video ("Journey to Islam") that he made with me in May 1997. It was to be followed by another video made on the present occasion ("New Approaches – New Millennium").

The event was coupled, as usual, with a near professional fund raising, which yielded close to US $500,000 – evidence of both the affluence and the spirit of sacrifice of the *ummah* in the United States.

And yet, I had misgivings throughout the journey because I do not wish to compete with other brothers and sisters *fī sabīlillāh*, nor do I want to feel like, or even become a "professional Muslim" who makes Islam his trade.

The Qur'ān: again and again

Istanbul, 22 October 1998

Three years ago, Şaban Kurt, owner and editor of an Islamic publishing house called Cağrı Yayınları (The Call) in Türbe-Istanbul, asked me to help him produce a German translation of the Qur'ān on the basis of the one that had appeared under the pseudonym of Max Henning (Leipzig, 1901). He had already republished the English translation by Marmaduke Pickthall and was also working on bringing out old French and Russian translations. His reasons for choosing the Henning version were convincing: it was no longer protected by copyright laws, and it was the only German translation of the Qur'ān done by a non-Muslim that Muslims considered to be adequate.

Little did I know what I was getting into when I said "yes". First, the old text had to be transcribed from Gothic into Latin script, and its verses had to be entirely renumbered because they still followed the obsolete numbering introduced by August Flügel in the 19th century. Then the Introduction and virtually all the footnotes turned out to be so anti- or un-Islamic that they had to be replaced. The Index was also inadequate because it was exclusively based on concepts nominally appearing in the text. (Thus, for instance, homosexuality was missing.)

That was not all. I belatedly realized that the German language had changed so much during the last century that many sentences could no longer be understood by Germans of today. (The Qur'ān is the only book whose language has remained standard for over 1400 years.) Finally, I had to Islamize the Henning translation in several crucial respects. I honoured his views provided that there was at least one Muslim commentator or translator who read a specific Qur'ānic passage in the same way. If this was not the case, I followed the Muslim consensus or majority view. If there was no majority view, in most (but not all) cases I followed Muhammad Asad's.

Given that I had to work with a Turkish secretary who did not know any German and without a German computer word programme, it took me altogether three years to produce the new edition. It began to be distributed today, even among Turkish Islamic Centres in Germany. (Another version, beautifully produced in Munich by Eugen Diederichs, was presented by myself during the Frankfurt Book Fair on 15 October 1999.)

If you think that I now believe I have been able to "master" the Qur'ān, you are mistaken.

Paying my respects to the Mahdī

Wad Madani, 10 March 1999

From 6 to 12 March, I was able to visit the Sudan, a much maligned and struggling country, too large to be seen in just a few days. I had been looking forward to meeting Hasan al-Turabi for a long time. Few people in the so-called "Third World" have as broad an education and are as brilliant communicators with the West as he. And yet, today, he is feared in Washington as Khartoum's "Grey Eminence" and a supporter of terrorism.

I saw what State terrorism really means when I visited the ruins of the Shifa Pharmaceutical Plant in the middle of Khartoum, destroyed, out of the blue, by American cruise missiles, without a thread of evidence of the alleged chemical weapons production. A stunning example of ruthless imperialism in the 20th century. Yet the Sudanese take it with a measure of wisdom and humour, blaming Monika Lewintzky, the Jewish lover of President Clinton, for his need to lash out.

Neither did I see any evidence of anti-Christianism while I was in Khartoum. On the contrary, I arrived an unforgivable thirty minutes late for breakfast with the German Ambassador because traffic was blocked by a Catholic procession... (By the way, my visa had also been issued by a Christian: the Sudanese Ambassador in Bonn.)

It is touching to see how simply the Mahdī, Muḥammad Aḥmad ibn 'Abd Allāh, and his successor had lived in Omdourman, and then to appreciate that the current Sudanese President resides in the very palace once used in 1885 by his arrogant opponent Charles Gordon.

I know of no other poor country whose small intellectual leadership is as highly educated as in the Sudan. Hasan al-Turabi is a leading Muslim activist, and with his courageous book *Women, Islam and Muslim Society* (1973) he has done more to re-establish the Islamic rights of Muslim women than anybody else. Nevertheless, meeting him for lunch on 8th March was a disappointment. I have the feeling that he has become so famous that he can no longer listen.

Today, in Wad Madani, 250 kilometres south of Khartoum, I visited a Qur'ānic School run exactly as it had been for 375 years: bright little boys who have come from all over Black Africa in order to spend several years at school are "adopted" by the leading *shaykh*. They get up every morning at 3 am in order to learn a new chapter of the Qur'ān and to write it down on their wooden slabs with self-made washable ink. Breakfast is served after the *fajr* prayer. Then they repeat what they had learned the day before. When it gets unbearably hot, in the afternoon, they take their siesta, and after the evening prayer they immediately go to bed. What a happy and cheerful group of children, with eyes wide-awake! I could ask any of the advanced students to recite whatever part of the Qur'ān I picked at random, and none of them ever failed the test.

Bait al-Qur'ān

Manama, 1 May 1999

It is not just money, but the single-minded devotion of Dr. Abdul Latif Jassim Kanoo that put Bahrain onto the map of countries holding Islamic heritage treasures. And it is here that the organization Discover Islam manages daily to convert Christian guest workers to Islam, most of them coming from the Philippines and India.

The Bait al-Qur'ān, a rare case of successful modern architecture in the Third World, inaugurated in 1990, now houses a unique collection of old manuscripts and translations of the Qur'ān, including a copy of the first Latin version, printed in 1543 in Basle at the suggestion of Martin Luther. It was revealing to see how the Latin translation – not bad at all – was sandwiched between anti-Islamic articles (e.g. by Melanchthon) in order to counteract any positive effect the reading might have.

Before my lecture, Dr. Kanoo proudly showed me his latest acquisition: an original copy of the second oldest German translation of the Qur'ān, by Johann Lange, printed in Hamburg in 1688. It is entitled *Complete Turkish Legal Code or Mahomet's Alkoran*, demonstrating that for the Germans, Islam used to be seen as the religion of their major foe, the Turks.

Thus, anti-Islamic feelings in Germany, related to the presence of Turkish guest workers, have a long, "solid" tradition.

"When the earth trembles..."

Istanbul, 17 August 1999

At 3:08 am, Turkey experiences the worst earthquake in a long time, reaching 7.8° on the Richter scale. The epicentre is near Gölçük, the Turkish naval base on the Marmara Sea near Izmit. My wife and I, fast asleep, are being thrown around in bed for forty-five endless seconds. There is no more electricity but the police call all citizens to leave their houses in expectation of a worse quake. So we spend the next few nights on an asphalted car park near our house – a scene weirdly resembling a picnic party.

I go around reminding people of what the 99th *sūrah* of the Qur'ān tell us: "When the earth trembles with her trembling, and the earth issues her burden, and people ask: 'What is happening with her?' On that day, she will recount what came to her knowledge. On that day, all people will come forward singly in order to be shown their deeds. Then, whoever has done an atom's weight of good, will see it; and whoever has done an atom's weight of evil, will see it." But none of my asphalt neighbours seems to have heard of such a *sūrah*. Kemalism has done away with such knowledge.

Soon, rumours started spreading about the fact that the naval base, where a high brass party had been going to celebrate the military's victory in the war against the *ḥijāb*, had been utterly destroyed by the quake and had even sunk into the sea. Had Gilles Kepel not called one of his books *The Revenge of Allah*?

For about a week, people in Istanbul walked about like zombies. Then life picked up again and they became as heedless (and as frequently saturated in rakı) as before. How many warnings do people need? How many warnings will they get?

Da'wah under coconuts

Kayamkulam, 12 February 2000

Muslims worldwide have an extremely relaxed attitude towards the notion of copyright. If a book is good for Islam, should it not reach as many people as possible, as cheaply as possible? In short, Muslims consider knowledge the property of all. Consequently, there exist "pirate copies" of virtually all my books, also in Malayalam, the language spoken in South India.

That is how I received an invitation from Cochin to speak to Muslims in Kerala, the southernmost State of India, on the Indian Ocean. The state was Islamized as early as the 8th century CE, not by conquest but through Arab traders led by Malik ibn Dinar. Today, Kerala has a relative Muslim majority, followed by Christians, Marxists, and Hindus – in that order.

The airport of Cochin has been cut out of an unending forest of coconut palms; one finds coconut palms all along the roads as well. The Muslim (male) Students' Organization of Kerala held its annual congress in Kayamkulam, situated between the arms of a river, and, of course, under coconut trees. 13,000 students attended. During my second lecture, totally unheard of during that season, it suddenly started to rain cats and dogs, and there was no escaping from it. When I nevertheless hesitated to continue, the student leader simply said: "Our guest speaker has come 6000 miles to speak to you. So please listen to him." Nobody budged. My manuscript disintegrated in the rain, the noise of which was louder than my voice through the loudspeakers. Yet, in perfect discipline, all the 13,000 students remained sitting where they were, dripping wet.

Afterwards, they showed me their book exhibition. Seeing that all the most famous people had been pirated, including Freud, Darwin, Nietzsche, and Sartre, I really could not complain; rather I started to feel honoured.

The only problem with my hosts, extremely hospitable like all Muslims, was their food. Everything tasted the same (like curry) and was so hot that it almost made me sick. Imagine, even their water was spiced! For the first time I felt like a damned American tourist when, at breakfast, I asked the waiter whether, perhaps, he had some rice crispies or cornflakes...

Fez versus Lahore

Lahore, 27 February 2000

As an admirer of Khurram Murad I was invited to Islamabad, Lahore and Karachi to deliver the first series of "Khurram Murad Memorial Lectures" for Khurshid Ahmad's Institute of Policy Studies.

Having recently visited the Red Fort in Delhi, when I saw the Red Fort of Lahore I was once again struck by the huge dimensions of such architectural marvels. How did Mogul emperors such as Jahangir, Shah Jahan and Aurangzeb reach such gigantic proportions, dwarfing the Ottoman Top Kapi Palace and Versailles? And how modest, in comparison, the tomb of Muhammad Iqbal, situated within the premises of the Lahore Fort!

There are jewels left in Lahore, such as the Shish Mahal (1631) and the Badshahi Mosque (1673), but one has the impression that India, a non-Muslim state, takes better care of its Islamic heritage than the Islamic Republic of Pakistan.

Worse, the old city of Lahore, which could rival Fez in medieval charm and cosiness, is so dirty and smelly that one cannot believe it is a Muslim city. Is not cleanliness one-third of our faith?

Ever since I have seen Akbar Ahmed's splendid film *Jinnah*, I understand that Pakistan, as an Islamic State, got off on the wrong foot, being founded by a great statesman, but not a great Muslim.

Burial in Istanbul

Istanbul, 5 April 2000

Z ekiye Ağralıgil, my mother-in-law, succumbed at 85 years of age to Alzheimer's disease. Today, she was buried in the enormous Kara Ahmed cemetery in Üsküdar. The burial prayer, which took place in the Teşvikiye mosque, presented the usual aspect: during the preceding *ẓuhr* prayer, slightly more than half the male participants hung around outside, talking and even smoking, thereby symbolizing the split between practising Muslims and passport Muslims in Turkey. Similarly, none of the women participated in the prayer, as if they had been counselled against that part of the ceremony as well. In addition, as is typical for Turkey and the Near East, many people coming for the burial wear disrespectful clothes such as jeans and gaudy shirts. Burial is no longer conducted as a dignified rite of passage.

At the same time, the fact that family members wash the corpse, carry the coffin to the hearse, and help dig the grave, implicates Muslims deeper in death than the Western departure ceremonies do. The latter have become so non-committal that when the coffin automatically disappears behind a curtain for cremation, one may easily fool oneself about the realities of death.

Even though they know that it is an illegitimate innovation (*bid'a*), Turkish *imāms* come to the house of the deceased to recite the Qur'ān and pray for about half an hour on the day of burial, as well as on the 8th and 40th day after. This helps to increase their remuneration and exposes people who would otherwise never be caught covering their hair or praying to a bit of religion. This fact somehow gives such *mevlüt* ceremonies a non-Islamic quality of magic (and keeps housewives busy in the kitchen when a bit of contemplation might be more appropriate).

Tell me how you handle your dead and I will tell you who you are.

Muhammad Asad's centennial

Vienna, 18 May 2000

Today, the Austrian Oriental Society Hammer-Purgstall organized a memorial on the occasion of Muhammad Asad's 100th birthday. He was born on 2 July 1900 in Lemberg – then Austrian, now Polish.

Thus, Austria began to rediscover one of her most important sons; the Muslim world, however, for whom Asad was Europe's gift of the century, failed to pay any attention. This was reflected in the fact that, except for myself, the other lecturers, Prof. Reinhard Schulze (Berne) and Günther Windhager (Vienna), and most of the audience were non-Muslims. Günther Windhager is currently writing his doctoral thesis on Asad – something unheard of so far in the Muslim world.

This phenomenon is not only based on thoughtlessness or ungratefulness, but it also reflects a lack of tolerance among Muslims. Somebody who wrote as much as Asad, and wrote such decisive books, covering all aspects of Islam – Qur'ān, *ḥadīth, fiqh*, and the recent history of Pakistan – cannot possibly find full acceptance. Indeed, one may not subscribe to certain aspects of Asad's translation and commentary of the Qur'ān, or appreciate his efforts to reduce the concept of *Sharī'ah* to mainly Qur'ānic norms, or his position on the *ḥijāb*, but does this diminish his enormous contribution to Islamic renaissance in the 20th century? Did anybody encourage

Western people to understand and adopt Islam more than him with his *Road to Macca*? Which other men of intellectual calibre in this century – Muhammad Iqbal, al-Mawdūdī, Ḥasan al-Bannā, Sayyid Quṭb, Fathi Osman, the Hathout Brothers, Rashid al-Ghannouchi, Anwar Ibrahim, Jeffrey Lang – promise to have a more lasting effect than Asad?

We do not have enough Muslim intellectuals to disregard our geniuses.

Index of Proper Names

Confucius, 9
Constantine the Great, 65

D
Delumeau, Jean, 156
Denffer, Ahmad von, 97, 98, 208
Dionysius Areopagita, 104, 105, 106, 121
Diouri, Mokhtar, 196

E
Eiff, Hansjörg, 205

F
Fahd b. 'Abd al-'Azīz, 204
Fārābī, al-, 28, 63
Farrakhan, Louis, 150
Fāṭimah, 152, 198
Franco, Francisco, 52
Freud, Sigmund, 3, 225
Frisch, Karl von, 3
Frost, Robert, 86
Fukuyama, Francis, 183

G
Gairdner, W.H.T., 106
Garaudy, Roger, 172
Ghannouchi, Rashid al-, 230
Ghazālī, Abū Ḥāmid al-, 27, 63, 105, 106, 107
Goldziher, Ignaz, 172
Gordon, Charles, 220
Grabar, Oleg, 7

Guénon, René, 172
Guillaume, A., 95

H
Ḥallāj, al-, 155
Hamidullah, Muhammad, 16, 17
Harnack, Adolf von, 117
Harris, Lis, 158
Hassan II, 191
Hathout (Brothers), 230
Hawking, Stephen, 180, 181
Hegel, Friedrich, 60, 87
Heisenberg, Werner, 182
Henning, Max, 217, 218
Herzog, Roman, 209, 210
Hobohm, Muhammad A., 91
Hofmann, J.C. Alexander, 47, 163
Horus, 121
Hume, David, 60, 123

I
Iblīs, 142
Ibn 'Arabī, 19, 28, 186
Ibn Hishām, 95
Ibn Isḥāq, 16, 95
Ibn Khaldūn, 59, 60, 61
Ibn Rushd, 27
Ibn Sa'ūd, 41, 144
Ibn Sīnā, 28, 63, 73
Ibrahim, Anwar, 230
Iqbal, Muhammad, 41, 138, 226, 230

Index of Subjects

148, 151, 152, 154, 155, 156,
166, 167, 171, 173, 186, 188,
189, 199, 208, 219, 221, 224
Hellenistic Christians, 118,
166
Judeo-Christians, 109, 137
Church of Jesus Christ of Latter-
Day-Saints. *See* Mormons
circumcision, 58, 100
cleanliness, 67, 140, 226
Communism, 86, 127, 128, 146,
175, 183, 211
consubstantiality, 65, 66, 155
cosmology, 106, 138, 169, 180
Council of American-Islamic
Relations (CAIR), 213
Council of Chalcedon, 155
Council of Ephesus, 65
Council of Nicaea, 65, 155, 173
2nd Vatican Council, 171

D

dār al-ḥarb, 55
dār al-Islām, 55
da'wah, 128, 216
Dayton Agreement, 206
demiurge, 27, 49, 106
democracy, 43, 109, 123, 124,
162, 207
dervish, 35, 50, 51, 114, 127, 143
devil, 141, 142, 202, 204
dhimmī. *See* minorities
Discover Islam, 221
divorce, 69, 112
Durūs al-Ḥasaniyya, 192

E

earthquake, 182, 222
economy, 38, 39, 70, 85, 109, 175

ecumenical movement, 171, 172
emanation, 106
equality of women, 112, 113
eschatology, 186
ethics, 4, 39
Evangel, 11, 36, 37, 77, 89, 117,
118, 137, 166, 171, 172, 189
evil eye, 101

F

fasting, 25, 29, 30, 46, 190
fatalism, 181
fate, 34, 101, 126, 128
fiqh. *See* law, Islamic
Front de Libération Nationale
(FLN), 14, 175, 177
Front Islamique du Salut (FIS),
176
fundamentalism, 63, 93, 94, 122,
123, 158
funeral, 144, 145
futuwwa, al-, 97

G

gnosticism, 105, 106, 107, 118,
121, 137, 154, 156, 169, 186
God, 6, 8, 10, 11, 15, 19, 23, 28,
32, 33, 34, 37, 44, 45, 46, 51,
54, 63, 65, 73, 88, 89, 101,
102, 103, 105, 106, 107, 109,
114, 115, 120, 121, 123, 125,
128, 132, 133, 134, 136, 140,
142, 143, 145, 155, 156, 157,
164, 166, 167, 169, 170, 173,
179, 180, 181, 187, 191, 200,
201, 203, 208
Gospel. *See* Evangel
Greens, 206

H

ḥadīth, 36, 40, 43, 68, 100, 138, 229
ḥāfiẓ, 50, 52
ḥajar al-aswad, al-. See Black Stone
ḥajj. See pilgrimage
Hasidic, 158
ḥijāb. See veil
Holy Ghost, 49, 106, 118, 155
holy war, 135, 184
human rights, 205, 207

I

'Ibāḍites, 177
Iblīs. *See* devil
Iconoclasticism, 8, 141
'Īd al-Aḍḥā, 203
'Īd al-Fiṭr, 57
ideology, 4, 110
ifṭār, 25, 191, 192
imām, 44, 54, 80, 151, 152, 169, 192
immanence, 187
incarnation, 133, 156, 157
international law, 55, 56
iqāma. See call to prayer
Islam, official recognition of, 97, 98
Islamic Information Service (IIS), 216
isrā', 145
Israel, 160, 161, 215

J

Jehovah, 45, 133
Jews, 75, 90, 95, 132, 133, 137, 158, 159, 161, 166, 189, 190, 206, 215

jihād. See holy war
jizyah. See poll tax

K

Ka'bah, 72, 73, 74, 160, 199, 200, 202
Kerala, 224
Kismet. See fate

L

Lahore, 226
law, Islamic, 24, 42, 55, 56, 80, 112, 123, 163, 164, 178, 229
Law of Nations. *See* international law
law, schools of, 98
light mysteries, 105, 106
Light Verse, 105
Logos, 11, 121

M

madhhab. See law, schools of
Madinah, Constitution of, 16, 95
Manichaeism, 34, 105
marriage, 79, 112, 136
Marxism, 4, 110, 224
materialism, 85, 86, 110
meditation, 140, 143
Mesnevi, 35
Mevlut, 76, 130, 228
Minā, 161, 202, 203, 204
minorities, 23
mi'rāj. See ascension
missionaries, 71, 127, 128
Mormons, 99
Mosques, 31, 54, 57, 58, 67, 86, 90, 112, 142, 143, 148, 151, 169, 175, 185, 186, 215, 226